The Shooting of Nancy Howard: A Journey Back to Shore

(A True Story)

By Alice Mathews

First published by Dog Ear Publishing
4011 Vincennes Rd
Indianapolis, IN 46268
www.dogearpublishing.net

ISBN: 978-1-4575-5460-5

This book is printed on acid-free paper.

Printed in the United States of America

For Eleanor and Bill

Contents

Prologue

At what point does an otherwise good man become overcome with evil? The Christian Bible tells us that Satan is like a beast that roams the earth looking for those he can destroy. Is a good man lost as soon as the beast's eyes light on him, or is there a point where there is still hope?

At what point does a good man become someone else? Is it when he looks across a casino floor and sees a woman whom he decides to approach, a less- than- beautiful woman with a voice that irritates most people? Surely Satan has better tools.

Perhaps it's when a man sees how easily millions of dollars can be diverted from an employer with a dubious reputation. Surely a few thousand here and there would not be missed. Perhaps stealing from such a person is not wrong. Then, if a few thousand dollars is not missed, a few million can just as easily be hidden by a smart man. Once the web of lust and greed has begun to be woven, how does even a good man escape?

How would a good man know that the price of hidden nights enjoying the body of a stranger could lead to the near death of the woman he had promised to love forever? Did it begin that first night? Is it possible to understand that a chance adventure, paid for by stolen dollars, would lead to his wife's blood trailing from her nearly destroyed face as she struggled to stay alive? Is there a point at which a man can accept what Satan offers and then say, "No more"? Can there be another David, who lusted and killed, and yet later became a man "after God's own heart"?

CHAPTER 1

The Nightmare Begins

Rain is rare in Dallas during the sweltering days of August. Maybe I should have sensed that the abnormal weather was a grim precursor to the explosion that would soon shatter my world. That Saturday began with no hint of the nightmare that was coming. Frank was out of town on one of his numerous and extended business trips to work with his rich client. I hoped he would call later, but I was happily anticipating the celebration at church that evening, when with my close friends, I would witness the baptism of their daughter.

The baptism ceremony ended with a brief reception and a picture taken of me with my friends. We then exchanged hugs, and I left to walk to my car in the church parking lot. Although light refreshments had been served at the reception, I was too busy celebrating with my friends to eat, so on the way home I decided to grab some dinner at Taco Bueno.

The rain had turned into a fine mist as I pulled into the driveway and pressed the button to open my garage door. Gathering my purse and bag of food, I got out of the car and headed toward the door to the house. Suddenly a strong arm grabbed me around the neck, and a deep, intimidating voice demanded my purse. My first thought was that this prank was not very funny. I whirled around to face the "prankster"— only to confront a stocky-looking man wearing a dark baseball cap and black-rimmed glasses. My brain registered only a brief awareness of his appearance because my focus immediately shifted to the barrel of a silver handgun aimed at my head.

"Gimmee your purse *now!*" the intruder repeated. In my flustered state, I handed him the bag of tacos. When expletives punctuated his third demand for my purse, I thrust it into his chest as I cried, "Jesus, save me." Then the bullet exploded into my head, directly over my left eye.

Sometime later—a few seconds or maybe several minutes—I became aware that I was partially lying across the top of the recycle bin. My first conscious thoughts—*You've been shot. You're gonna die!*—were subdued by the sound of a voice saying, "Get up! Get up!" Reaching to the metal stand beside the bin, I managed to pull myself to a partial standing position, for a moment. But my legs buckled, sending me face down onto the concrete. My efforts to get up again were futile—the blood-slick floor made regaining my footing impossible. At that point, I began spitting out bloody tissue , and I resorted to belly- crawling toward the car. Somehow I opened the door and reached for the steering wheel to pull myself back into the car. If I can just reach the ONSTAR medical alert button to call for help. No help there, maybe because I pushed the wrong button or because I needed the key to get through to someone—and the key was in my stolen purse.

I believed I was about to die. But the memory of that voice ordering me to get up urged me on. Leaning on the car hood, I began staggering through my own blood toward the door to the house, fighting not to slip on the concrete floor. I considered that my attacker might be lurking in the driveway to take another shot at me, so I hit the button to close the garage door. Inside the house, I stumbled into the laundry room to turn off the burglar alarm. A little late for that. But for some reason I dreaded hearing the shrill blare of the alarm. Although I could barely make out the numbers, I was finally able to enter the right code to disarm the security system.

That small success was enough to move me a few more steps—into the bathroom adjacent to the laundry room. The mirror reflected a gruesome image—my body covered with blood from my head down. I grabbed a fluffy white towel to stop the bleeding, but it quickly starting leaking red droplets on the floor. Holding the towel against the side of my head and trying to ignore the trail of blood behind me, I shuffled into the kitchen and reached for the landline. I just needed to push three little numbers—911. Another success.

The next challenge? Talking, making myself understood. The police dispatcher, a woman whom I later learned was Dustie, managed to comprehend my plea for help, despite my gasping for breath and the gurgling blood in my throat. In fact, I was able to tell her I had been shot, give her my name and location, and describe the shooter—in between crying out to Jesus to save me. Dustie calmed me as much as possible, assuring me that the police and emergency personnel were on the way, and promising to stay on the phone with me until they arrived. *No one wants to die alone.*

When she asked if I could open the front door, I answered by nodding my head. Knowing help was on the way enabled me to reach the door, unlock it, and then sit in a chair to await the arrival of help.

As I sat there in the foyer for what seemed a lifetime, I looked through the glass pane of the front door. A flash of yellow caught my eye. I tried to focus on that flash when abruptly a hand extended from what seemed to be a yellow jacket. No...no...no.... The hand was holding a gun that was aimed at the door. Panic gripped me. The attacker had returned to finish me off!

Once again, Dustie calmed me, explaining that the hand and the gun I saw belonged to a police officer and that I should open the door. Shaking with fear, I complied and to my relief faced two police officers on the porch with guns drawn in case the attacker was inside. They asked me to step outside the door, where medical responders had positioned a gurney and were ready to wheel me into an ambulance. Before I made it to the gurney, I fell, into the arms of a police officer, as I was later told. I vaguely remember hearing the siren of the ambulance, the feeling of a cervical collar being placed around my neck, and one of the paramedics telling me that he was about to give me something for the pain. My last memory of that ride to Parkland Hospital is of my screams as he poked a needle between my toes.

In the trauma center at Parkland, doctors determined that I had extensive damage to my head, and damaged nerves along the path of the bullet, which was lodged in my right lung; a fractured rib, and fractures to my neck. Doctors had the tedious job of suturing torn flesh around my eye, sinuses, and throat; as well as repairing my hard palate.

While the doctors were working to repair as much damage to my body as possible, the police remained at my house and began their investigation. One of the officers knew me as a member of his church and called my pastor, Dr. Brent Taylor, who contacted my other close friends and family. One of my daughters called Frank, her father and my husband of almost thirty years. Due to hospital protocol in criminal cases, however, my family was unable to get information about my condition. In fact, I had even been admitted under a false name. After several frantic hours, my son called a family friend, a Carrollton police officer who intervened with the hospital to release information about my condition to family members.

Those first few days in the ICU unit were filled with endless rounds of medication (usually injected) and hourly neurological tests, as well as the wretched breathing tube that had been inserted through my mouth during the ambulance ride. And then there was that vile cervical collar that ensured I could find no comfortable position. I felt like a prisoner in my own body. I couldn't talk, could barely move, and was constantly hot. My hands had been tied down to stop me from pulling at the breathing tube. I resorted to using sign language, to get ice to cool my body, a request that my daughters could convey to the nurses.

I was sometimes aware of others in the room—various doctors and nurses, my mother, our two daughters, our son, and Frank. I hung on to the knowledge that I was surrounded by the love of so many family members and friends, but especially my Lord, who had given me back my life when I thought it was slipping away. I was heartened when I heard Frank whispering softly in my ear, "Honey, we're going to get through this together." Maybe my close brush with death would reawaken the affection that we seemed to have lost during the last two or three years. If so, all of this suffering might lead to a stronger marriage, like the one we had had years ago.

CHAPTER 2

Happier Times

Remembering six years ago, my forty-fifth birthday—what surprise would Frank spring on me this year? It would be hard to top my fortieth celebration when he had told me to pack a bag for both cold and warm weather—that we would be leaving in ten days for a weeklong trip. No worries about the kids: He had already arranged for my mother to house- sit and oversee their comings and goings. A long flight to Vancouver was followed by a taxi ride to the pier where a huge cruise ship was moored. That trip to Alaska was spectacular! Precious memories of the breathtaking glaciers and the booming sounds of their calving; our laughter when an unexpected wave sprayed Frank's camera as he was about to capture the perfect picture of a whale breaching close to our boat. And then there was the ring that kept drawing me back to a little store in Juneau as we meandered through the little shops along the pier. It was much too expensive, but Frank overrode my objections and bought it anyway.

So as I was approaching the midpoint of my fortieth year, would Frank still care enough to plan a special surprise for me? Grabbing a second cup of coffee on his way out the door, he tossed an envelope on the kitchen table. "Happy early birthday," he murmured and kissed the top of my head. Then he quickly headed to the garage and to his day at the office. Should I go ahead and open the envelope even though my birthday is tomorrow? I wonder. Curiosity won out, of course. There was a birthday card inside, in my favorite color: purple. The sentiment was sweet, but even sweeter were the two tickets to the Barry Manilow concert on Saturday night. What a sacrifice! Frank had shelled out big bucks for two tickets. I hoped he would use the second ticket and not send one of the kids with me. (Barry's appeal seemed to have missed Frank.)

When he came home that evening, I hugged him and began singing, "I can't smile without you."

Laughingly, he replied, "I guess you like your present."

"Absolutely! As long as the tickets are for both of us."

"You bet. I think I can deal with Barry for a couple of hours."

The concert was as exciting as I had hoped, especially with the frenzy of mostly female fans screaming Barry's lyrics with him and waving their lit-up phones. Even more memorable was the drive home, as Frank and I sang together, "I feel sad when you're sad/ I feel glad when you're glad." Then we joined our voices to harmonize on the anthem we would be singing in the choir on Sunday, "Light of the City." I was flooded by so many memories of singing together our favorite songs, many of which are hymns. That was a special night that I will always remember.

Nancy and Frank Howard

It was the summer of 2008. Frank again proved himself to be the master of surprises. One evening at dinner he announced that he was taking our family of five, along with his parents, to the Olympics in Beijing. I was astounded! "How can we afford that?" Frank then revealed that for months he had been saving for this experience, and he had made all the arrangements—flights, hotels, tickets to venues. So, in August, we were off on the best and last family trip we would ever take.

The next summer, I planned a trip, this time to take our younger daughter with me on a mission trip to Zambia. Along with other church members, we were to work with orphaned children, most of whom had lost their parents to the AIDS epidemic that had swept several villages in the area. Even children with living relatives were left on their own and treated as trash. I became heartsick by what I saw—little waifs in tattered rags that barely covered their emaciated bodies.

Through several interpreters, we taught the children songs about Jesus, a name they seemed never to have heard before. They especially loved all the hand and body motions that accompanied the songs. Despite their desperate living conditions, those children were like children everywhere. They loved to squirm and wiggle and make funny gestures. But I noticed that one of the little girls in my group would stand by herself. Her eyes seemed vacant, and her face registered no emotion. She didn't join in on any of the singing; in fact, I wondered if perhaps she was deaf and mute. The only way she was engaged in anything that the group would do was when the children sat down for the meal we provided: two slices of bread, a protein drink, and a piece of fruit—the only food most of them would have for the entire day. She ate her lunch but with no evidence of pleasure.

The pastor in a nearby village explained that the little girl, Eneles, showed signs of being possessed by demons. Evidently demon possession was thought to be a common malady among the people in this area. One evening, our church team was asked to participate in a prayer service to save Eneles. We formed a circle around her, prayed over her, and then called on the name of Jesus. After a few minutes Eneles started shaking violently, her eyes rolled back in her head, and she fell backward. The pastor raised her to a sitting position and asked how she felt. When she complained that her stomach hurt and she couldn't breathe well, we repeated the prayers and called on the name of Jesus. After this second period of intense prayer, she felt fine and began acting like a normal child. She even prayed to receive Jesus on the final night.

As we prepared to leave the village at the end of the week, we were delighted to furnish each child with a pair of new shoes and socks—the first substantial footwear most of them had ever had. But the gifts that I received from those children would not wear out like those shoes: the gifts of gratitude to God for all His blessings, the firsthand knowledge that the name of Jesus has great power, and the desire to share the love of God with others—*these are gifts that I hope I never outgrow.*

As our plane began its landing at DFW, my daughter and I grew more excited to be home. As we exited customs with our luggage, Frank was waiting to welcome us. He hugged us both, loaded up our luggage, and began driving to our house. My daughter and I were bursting with stories about our experiences, especially seeing firsthand the miraculous power of God in that dark, impoverished country. Suddenly I noticed Frank's shoulders begin to shake and tears run down his face. "Frank, pull over to the shoulder. You're in no shape to drive," I said. Thankfully, he slowed down and turned into the driveway of a motorcycle dealership. By this time, Frank's tears had escalated, he had his head in his hands, and he was sobbing, obviously grief-stricken about some devastating news.

My daughter and I grew more alarmed. Frank almost never shed a tear, and he had never before wept with his whole body that I had seen. Gradually, his sobs subsided, and he told us that a very close family friend, someone who had been a grandfather figure to our children, had suddenly died from an aneurysm. I shared Frank's grief at this news, but I couldn't help but wonder at the dramatic effect the man's passing had on Frank. His response seemed so out of character, but then maybe, I thought, as we age we become more disturbed by death, especially that of someone so close to our family.

When we got home and I was unpacking, I glanced at the dresser and saw my cell phone, which in my haste I had left behind. As I played the messages that I had missed, my eyes teared up. One message was from our friend, telling me he was in the hospital. I would always regret that I heard his message only after he had gone on to be with the Lord.

CHAPTER 3

Travel Woes and Fraying Marriage

A few months after my trip to Africa, Frank let me know that our expensive trip to China had only been the first of many extravagances that we could now afford. He had a new client who had become rich through defense department contracts to furnish ice to troops stationed in Iraq. Richard Raley, this new client, wanted Frank to help him bring millions of dollars into the United States from Kuwait. Moreover, Raley would provide Frank with an office in Grapevine, Texas, as well as the use of his private jet.

This mother lode could change our lives for the better although it would also require Frank to travel quite a bit. But somehow I couldn't share his enthusiasm, mainly because he had made the decision without ever consulting me. In the past, we had always discussed important issues before deciding on how to handle them, even talking about the pros and cons of buying a Lexus. And now, almost out of the blue, Frank had agreed to accept a client whose demands might well change our lives.

Frank's work for Raley soon morphed into an even more lucrative position when he became the company's chief financial officer. Out-of-town trips were becoming the norm rather than the exception, even trips over the weekend. His frequent absences made it impossible for me to make plans for any kind of date night. One evening, as he was packing a suitcase to leave for his next trip, I brought the calendar into the room and asked him to commit to a weekend so that we could do something special together, just the two of us. When he protested that he couldn't say for certain which days he would be in town, I angrily hurled the calendar across the room and yelled, "I am sick and tired of never being able to plan anything," and I stomped out the door.

The next morning after a restless night, I awoke to find Frank preparing to leave for his trip. He informed me that he had a meeting in California with Richard Raley and would probably be gone for at least four or five days. "Why can't you work with Raley here in town?" I asked.

"I just can't. I'll call you with my flight information as soon as I know when I'll be back." A quick peck on the cheek, and he was out the door, leaving me with unspoken accusations of the Raley account becoming the "other woman."

. . . .

As Frank's fiftieth birthday approached in the fall of 2009, I began thinking of ways to celebrate the milestone. He was adamantly against any kind of party or celebration; in fact, he said he would rather just ignore the day altogether. Nevertheless, I was determined to show him how important and special he still was to me.

I came up with the idea of giving him fifty things each day, starting with the fifty days before his birthday. I searched the house and scoured the Internet for practical ideas—fifty rubber bands, fifty paper clips, fifty ways to say "I love you." For the days when he was traveling, I packed the items into his suitcase. The day before his birthday, I presented him with fifty items of clothing—such as socks, underwear, and shirts. And then, on his birthday, I gave him an envelope full of fifty or more cards from friends, family, and clients. In retrospect, I had amused myself by imagining reactions to finding all these items during his trips.

But his trips become more and more frequent and prolonged. Because Raley's company had begun shipping military supplies over to Iraq and Afghanistan, Frank was periodically required to travel to the Kuwait office. I understood the demands of Frank's CFO role, that trips abroad were part of the job. But I suspected that these demands accounted for only some of Frank's numerous absences. Raley's wealth had provided him the opportunity and the means to enjoy extravagant forms of entertainment and pleasure: world-class golf courses, executive suites at sporting events, expensive restaurants and resorts—the best of everything. And Frank was enjoying all of this at Richard's expense.

I soon found myself living the life of a single woman. When Frank did come home, it was usually for just a few days. His suitcase was almost always open for unpacking or repacking. (I had come to hate that suitcase—for me, it represented what had gone terribly wrong in our marriage, the mistress that had stolen my husband.)

On one rare occasion, Frank was home long enough for us to go to a concert by one of our favorite bands, Chicago. As the band performed, I was reminded of the good times in our marriage, back when we had listened to and sung many of these same songs. Nostalgia moved me to sing again. I reached over to pull Frank's face toward me and began singing in his ear,

"You're my inspiration." Abruptly, he jerked away from me and seemed to shake his head in disgust. The wound from that response still hurts.

Still, I refused to abandon hope. Maybe marriage counseling would provide some avenue of recovering our marriage. At first, I went by myself, but later Frank agreed to go with me. In one of our dual appointments, the counselor bluntly asked Frank if he was having an affair. His answer was a resounding "No!" However, in my mind I answered back, "His mistress is Richard Raley."

Counseling provided no panacea, but it did inadvertently lead to a temporary pause in Frank's travels. At the counselor's suggestion that Frank get a medical checkup, he reluctantly made an appointment. But on the day of the appointment, he told me that the doctor had had to cancel and would reschedule; then later he told me that he had rescheduled. "So, which is it? Did you or the doctor reschedule?" I demanded to know. I had become so angry at the inconsistencies, at the lies. When Frank said that he had rescheduled, I asked for the date and the time; then I wrote it on the calendar. I was determined not to let him change his mind. Furthermore, I was going to go with him.

After his second doctor's appointment, which followed several medical tests, Frank learned that he had prostate cancer and would require over eighty sessions of radiation. As we were about to walk out the door, the doctor leaned over and told me, "You probably saved his life by insisting that he get a checkup."

For the next few months, Frank went five days a week, every week, for radiation. Forced to stay in town, Frank seemed less aloof and more attentive to me. I wondered if his illness had made him more sympathetic to me and my many years of struggling with fibromyalgia and chronic fatigue. I was determined to walk this journey with him. Unfortunately, the end of his radiation also marked the end of this brief respite from the discord in our marriage.

With Frank's victory over cancer, his travel resumed in earnest. And now his indifference to me sometimes even descended into outright hostility. I kept asking myself what I had done to justify this radical shift in his behavior. With no clear answer to that question, I thought that maybe this was just a "midlife crisis on steroids." We were living in two different worlds with no common ground. That realization was highlighted by the flagrant lies he would often tell about his location.

Once when he was scheduled to fly into DFW from Kuwait, I decided to surprise him by meeting him at the airport. I waited outside customs for over an hour after the flight arrived, but still there was no Frank. I then called his office to ask when he was scheduled to return from Kuwait. Raley's wife informed me that he and Richard had really returned the week before, but Frank had gone on to California. For two more days, I heard nothing from Frank. When he finally came home, supposedly from Kuwait, I asked to see his boarding pass. "I don't have it," he replied. "I left it on the plane." To my demand to know where he had been, he had no answer.

. . . .

After all the conflict over Frank's mysterious travels, he surprised me in the summer of 2011. The church was planning another trip to Zambia to do mission work. Our younger daughter wanted us to participate, but this time she cajoled Frank into going along as well. On the trip, Frank seemed to enjoy working with the young boys and with our daughter. We also met other couples with whom we had several interesting conversations, and once, somehow the topic of becoming "empty-nesters" came up. One of the couples suggested that starting a new hobby together was a good strategy for transitioning to becoming only a couple again. They were especially enthusiastic about their own hobby, taking dancing lessons.

When we returned home, I asked Frank if he would be willing to take dancing lessons with me. To my surprise, he said yes. When we arrived at our first class, I was surprised again: The class was for dancing in the round. Even though we didn't know exactly what that meant, we decided to enroll. We quickly learned that in circle dancing, there is a caller, much like in square dancing, but instead of changing partners, we would dance with the same partner, sometimes side by side, holding hands, and sometimes facing each other in a circle with the men inside the circle and the women on the outside.

I soon discovered that Frank was a much better dancer than I was, even though he had never danced in college. He became very adept at dodging my feet, which at times threatened to trip us both to the floor. I think this kind of dancing suited him because it was methodical, like Frank himself. We had to keep up with the number of steps for each move, which I continued to get confused. But Frank, the CPA, was very good at numbers, so he always seemed to know just how many steps to take.

Dancing with Frank was exhilarating, making me feel young and carefree again. So, for every Tuesday night until July 2012, when the teachers ended the class, we were dancing in circles. In fact, Frank enjoyed it so much that he arranged his travel so that he could leave on Wednesdays and be home on Monday nights.

In the spring of 2012, I was inspired by a sermon preached by a visiting minister at our church. I needed to find a way to recapture the close spiritual connection that Frank and I had shared in the past. I asked Frank whether he would be willing to get up early with me before he went to work so that we could pray and read the Scriptures together. When he agreed, I was encouraged. I even bought two copies of a devotional book for us to read together, even when he was traveling. We decided that we would take turns choosing a devotion for each of us to read and then we would share our thoughts about it either by phone or by text. For a few weeks, we continued to start our mornings in this way, but gradually Frank's early meetings began to interrupt this special form of communication.

To relieve some of my loneliness, friends suggested that I get a dog. After all, our three children were now gone from the home, and I was largely by myself in a big house. The nest had never felt so empty. At first, I hesitated, thinking of all the responsibility of caring for a pet. But, finally, out of desperation for companionship, I searched the Internet and found a puppy that had been bred to be a lapdog, something I could cuddle. The breeder agreed to fly the puppy from Alabama to Dallas. The three-month-old ball of fur arrived safely and, though dazed at first, quickly became my little shadow. Because it was close to Christmastime, I considered her to be my Christmas gift to myself, my little Joy-Noel.

Though Joy-Noel brought a new warmth to the house, I was becoming increasingly anxious about the distance growing between Frank and me. Our marriage seemed to be falling apart. Several months earlier I had decided to become more proactive in salvaging our relationship. The upcoming new year would be the perfect time for us to reignite the love we had shared for over twenty-eight years. After confirming with Frank that he would be in town on New Year's Eve, I made reservations for dinner at a mystery theater, which would be followed by a midnight celebration. As December 31 approached, I decided to welcome the new year with a new outfit: a new dress, jewelry, shoes, the works. I wanted to look my best for our special evening.

A few days before New Year's Eve, as he was leaving for the office, Frank informed me that he would be going to New York to celebrate the new year with Richard. And furthermore, he would be staying over for a couple of days for a New Year's Day football game. After dropping that bombshell, he was out the door without another word. *Frank never liked confrontation*, I realized. Had he slapped me in the face, I could not have been more hurt, angry, bewildered, brokenhearted. I ended one year and began the next—in despair.

CHAPTER 4

Wounds and Losses

As I lay in the ICU, Frank's reassurance, "We'll get through this together," calmed me back to sleep. I needed to shut out the memory of my bloody reflection in the bathroom mirror. My next conscious thought was one of confusion. What is that blurry shape at the foot of the bed? The shape began moving toward me, gradually revealing the welcomed sight of my husband. As he held my hand, Frank whispered the devastating news that my eye had been destroyed by the bullet and would have to be surgically removed. Unable to vocalize my shock because of the breathing tube that was down my throat, my brain repeated, Oh no, oh no, oh no! That just can't happen. I can't lose an eye."

Not only did I mourn the physical trauma and disabling condition that would result from that loss, but I also grieved over losing the feature that had so often generated compliments and comparisons to Elizabeth Taylor's eyes. But two days after the shooting, the eye surgeon performed the removal. I later learned that the trauma to my eye had been so severe that the surgeon had difficulty even distinguishing between the tissue and my eye. He told me that I was fortunate to still have an eyelid.

That loss was just the beginning. I still had to face a significant loss of movement in my right arm and hand, which required intense and painful bouts of therapy to restore. Even after the breathing tube was removed, I was unable to eat or drink because of the extensive damage to my mouth, throat, and esophagus. My nourishment had to come from an IV. To relieve the dryness in my mouth, the nurses gave me small, wet sponge sticks. I was also informed that I had suffered a collapsed lung, an injury that amazed several medical personnel because I had still been able to direct paramedics to the house. I hoped that at least my voice would eventually heal enough that I could sing again. Thankfully, God spared me that gift.

The physical damage I suffered was accompanied by the trauma of fear. When the blinds in my hospital room were opened, I was terrified that someone might see me and shoot me again. The first time I left my room, I was wheeled down to the X-ray department for a feeding test. The doctors wanted to see how my throat would function when I tried to swallow.

As the orderly pushed my wheelchair, I began to shake, fearing that an attacker was just around the corner, ready to finish me off.

Miracles from God sustained me as I became more aware of my injuries and my close brush with death. The voice that had urged me to get up from the garage floor; my ability to walk into the house, turn off the security system, call 911 for help, and stagger to the front door—all the while bleeding profusely and struggling for breath—all that could be explained only by God's power. In fact, one of the detectives who studied the crime scene commented that, given the profusion of blood in the garage and the house, he was amazed I had survived. With all the damage that my body suffered, I was only alive because the bullet, shot point-blank into my face, traveled downward, only grazing my brain; away from my spinal cord, jugular vein, carotid arteries, vocal cords, esophagus, and heart. It finally lodged in my right lung, where it remains to this day. And so do I.

Over the next few days, I was overwhelmed by the flood of calls, cards, and visits from my church family and other friends and relatives. So many people came to the hospital that the nurses had to begin restricting the number of visits so that I could get the rest I needed. One visitor, Frank, was suddenly missing after he had been at my bedside that first morning in the hospital. Finally, on the third day, he called. He called not to tell me he was on his way to the hospital but to admit that he had been having an affair, which had lasted almost three years. So, I had been right all along. He did have a mistress, but it turned out to be an actual woman, in California, not his work for Richard Raley, which I had suspected of being the "other woman."

I soon learned that Frank's admission of adultery was prompted not by guilt but by necessity. The police detectives had immediately started investigating the attack. They had seized the computers and cell phones from our home, as well as all computers and phones connected with Frank's work as a CPA. They very quickly discovered e-mails, photos, phone calls, and records of bank transactions that signaled a clear message: Frank had been involved with a woman in California for over three years.

Frank had met the woman, Suzanne Leontiff, at a casino in Lake Tahoe during the time I was first in Africa. Suzanne, a dental hygienist and the mother of two daughters, had been separated from her husband and lived in Santa Cruz. Apparently, after that first meeting, Frank and Suzanne had been in constant communication and began arranging time to be together. The relationship developed quickly, as I was to learn later; so quickly, in fact, that Frank used his position with Raley to finance increasingly expensive gifts for

Suzanne: trips to softball tournaments for her daughters, to professional ballgames, and to the Bahamas; a boat; a house in Santa Clara; and a condo in Lake Tahoe. He started an IRA for her, in addition to giving her close to a million dollars in cash, and money for the education of one of her daughters. According to Richard Raley, Frank financed all of these extravagances with money he had skimmed from the company's government contracts.

Beyond the outrageous sums that Frank had spent on this woman and her children, I was wounded by various items that the detectives discovered in his office: a picture of Frank with Suzanne and her daughters in a frame that had the word *Love* across the top, and a Mother's Day card he had given her that was addressed "to my wife." In fact, I learned that one Mother's Day Frank had sent flowers to Suzanne and to her mother; to me and to my mother; and to his own mother. Was he in some subconscious way trying to combine these disparate parts of his life? In my pain and heartache, I was further bewildered when I learned he had signed the papers on the house for Suzanne—on my birthday. Evidence of other significant dates for our family were also the same dates he had showered Suzanne and her girls with gifts.

As details of the three-year affair continued to come out, more incriminating evidence began to surface. In their search of our house and Frank's office, the detectives also uncovered e-mails, cell phone conversations, and bank transactions that connected Frank to a shady family of criminals. The patriarch of that family was Billie Earl Johnson. That connection was to be the thread that would ultimately untangle a bizarre network of individuals who had been involved in my shooting.

About six days after the shooting, detectives told me that they had substantial evidence to arrest Frank on suspicion of murder-for-hire. A couple of days later, Frank was arrested and jailed, fueling a huge flurry of media attention. As an active and longtime member of the largest Baptist church in Carrollton, Texas, Frank was known in the community as a man of unimpeachable character, a strong Christian, an upstanding businessman, and a devoted family man. How could such a man abandon all the principles that had previously governed his life and essentially live a double life for three years? How could the husband who had vowed to forsake all others but me, embezzle money to support a mistress and then hire someone to kill me? These questions continued to plague me, sometimes haunting me with the uncertainty of whether I had ever really known him.

CHAPTER 5

The Bail Hearing

Frank's arrest galvanized a roller coaster of conflicting news and emotions—at first, our family's disbelief of Frank's guilt. Then the police told us that Frank had confessed to the murder-for-hire-charge. But no, a few hours later we learned that the police had forced his confession. But no, what really happened—someone else on a different case had confessed. I was physically, mentally, and emotionally exhausted. All I could muster was a silent prayer: *Lord, please reveal the truth and strengthen me to live with whatever it turns out to be.*

Dealing with that truth had to be postponed while I began the arduous journey of rebuilding my body, which would be a painful process. I often thought of how God had provided a positive use for my fibromyalgia: I was already accustomed to intense pain. As my pastor has often declared, "God wastes nothing." The doctors cleared me to move to a rehab hospital, the location of which had to remain confidential. The threat to my life was still a very real possibility.

The decision to move my location came with no warning. Suddenly, I was being taken from my room to an ambulance, then leaving for some location that I didn't know. I had no phone, no way to contact anyone. Again, I was overwhelmed by anxiety. My one comfort was being able to wear my own clothes.

Once in physical therapy, I spent three hours a day subjected to painful exercises to help me function with one eye and to regain movement in my arm. One of the exercises for my arm and hand involved "walking" my fingers up and down a hand ladder. On one occasion, another patient beside me was working with weights, and the weights fell, making a loud noise. The sound, as loud as the gunshot had been, frightened me so much that my knees buckled, and I fell into a chair weeping. I also experienced various cognitive struggles that led the doctor to order brain retraining therapy. That therapy was added to my rigorous daily physical therapy.

While rehab was consuming so much of my days, Frank's bookkeeper, along with our children, began preparing for Frank's bail hearing. They solicited letters of support from friends and other family members, expressing confidence in Frank's good character. At the hearing, there was standing room only, with over sixty people attending to show their solidarity with Frank. Several of his supporters even offered to help pay his bail, which was set at one million dollars.

At the hearing, however, the lead detective laid out the evidence justifying the huge bail. He testified that in early 2010 Frank had contacted a convict named Billie Earl Johnson, whom he hoped he could hire to kill me. In his conversations, both then and later, Frank used his first name, John. (His given name is John Franklin.) Ironically, I heard later how Frank had learned about Billie. Frank worked as the CPA for a company where Billie's former girlfriend also worked. When she broke up with Billie, he started harassing her, so Frank called Billie, purportedly to warn him to leave her alone. When I learned about this at the hearing, I remember at the time thinking, *Frank always avoids confrontation.* In our history, Frank had never shown any inclination to be a "white knight in shining armor," as he appeared to have been for Billie's ex-girlfriend.

The detective testified that Frank (that is, John) drove to Mesquite, Texas, to meet Billie Earl at a western wear store. There he handed Billie an envelope with sixty thousand dollars in cash and a photograph of me. According to Billie, Frank instructed him to make the hit "look like an accident." Billie and his new girlfriend, Stacey Serenko, quickly burned through that money—buying drugs, shopping, and handing out hundred-dollar bills. The detective explained that that initial meeting was only the first of several meetings, in which Billie asked for and received more payments of several thousand dollars each. At one meeting, Stacey took a picture of Frank, and later she sent it to her mother...just in case.

Other unsavory characters related to Billie in various ways began to offer their services, promising Frank to deliver on his request for my murder. Each time Frank would hand over money or transfer funds through bank transfers to their bank accounts—without ever getting the result he was paying for. He would meet them at public places: a Walmart, a shopping mall, a Grandy's restaurant, and so on.

On one occasion, Frank met with Stacey's son, Dustin Hiroms. At that time, Billie and Stacey were both in jail, which provided Dustin the opportunity to get in on the action. Frank told Dustin that I would be attending a three-day conference at the Gaylord Texas Hotel in Grapevine, Texas. That location would be ideal for the hit, Frank said, but Dustin should use a bat or a knife, not a gun, which would draw too much attention. The detective then confirmed that I had, indeed, attended that conference.

Frank countered these accusations with the assurance that this cast of criminals were extorting money from him. When he finally refused any further payments, they threatened to go through with it and kill me—saying they knew where I lived and what kind of car I drove. He then explained that he wasn't at liberty to say any more until the trial.

The hearing ended with the judge upholding the million-dollar bail, for which Frank had to pay one hundred fifty thousand dollars. He was released but required to wear an ankle monitor and ordered to stay away from me and from our house. While on bail, Frank stayed with his older brother in Ponder, Texas, but he would drive every day to his CPA firm, located in Dallas.

In addition to the criminal charges that Frank was facing, Richard Raley filed a lawsuit against him, accusing Frank of setting up shadow companies to siphon millions of dollars from Raley accounts in Kuwait into bank accounts in Frank's name. Ironically, Frank allegedly named those companies with versions of Suzanne's names, one being SLH—the initials for Suzanne Leontieff-Howard if they were to marry and another named Sutaho (combining the names Suzanne and Tahoe). Police estimated the dollar amount of the embezzlement at some thirty-eight million dollars; they also alleged that Frank wired money from one of those accounts (the Genshu Management Company) to a person he was hoping to hire for the hit.

With this whirlwind of suits and countersuits, my lawyer recommended that I protect my financial health by filing for divorce, thereby freezing the assets comprising our community property. I also wanted to ensure that our assets wouldn't get tied up in attorneys' fees. To prevent the divorce filing from implying my belief in Frank's criminal guilt, I included this statement in it: "The decision to file for divorce does not express a conviction of my husband's guilt in the manner of criminal solicitation, but is the required response to my husband's infidelity and deception where our joint finances are involved." The grounds for the divorce were listed as "discord or conflict of personalities, as well as adultery."

CHAPTER 6

New Body, Persistent Fears

A little over a month after the shooting, the doctors determined that I was making enough progress in using my arm, as well as in strengthening my body and balance, that I was ready for outpatient therapy. That meant it was time to go home. But *home* no longer meant a place of comfort, security, or love. Now it triggered a rush of fear and panic. Even the thought of going back to that house, that garage, made me nauseous. I was oddly relieved when the detectives told me that returning to the crime scene could be dangerous. They explained that there was still a network of people capable of "finishing the job." Therefore, they wanted me to move to a secret location, where only a few of my closest family members and maybe a few close friends would know.

I considered several possible places to go. A close friend offered to have me stay in a gated community with her and her teenage daughter, but I feared that my presence might endanger them. Perhaps I could move to an apartment or hotel; however, I needed to be frugal with my money. After much thought and prayer, I decided to ask my youngest brother whether my mother and I could move in with him. Although he was single, the logistics were far from ideal, especially since he already had a couple from church and their daughter as temporary house guests. However, we all managed, thanks to my brother's camping out in the living room and letting my mom and me have his room.

For someone who valued his privacy, my brother was remarkably patient in tolerating four women in his house—makeup, bras, pantyhose, perfume, and all. He would continue to be a huge help to me in the months to come, making trips to my house for things I needed, advising me on financial matters, putting a knob on my car's steering wheel so I could more easily turn it with my injured arm. I will always be grateful to him for helping me resume my life.

On my first full day out of rehab, I had to go to Denton, Texas, for the court hearing connected to the divorce. The purpose of the hearing was to agree on the division of community assets. Although I dreaded this hearing, I was looking forward to being out of the hospital, dressing up, and finally wearing makeup again. Dressing myself was still difficult because of my injured arm, but even more challenging was applying eye makeup. I discovered that applying eyeliner requires one to close that eye, but if it's the only eye you have, the process is quite comical, not to mention the result. After several attempts, I learned to open my eye just a bit, so I could see where I was putting the eyeliner. As for the other eye (or where that eye had been), the doctors had sewn together my eyelids. I had to be content to simply add a bit of eyeshadow.

Along with my mother and brother, I arrived at the courthouse, where I met my attorneys. Frank was already there with his parents and lawyers. After several attempts by the attorneys to find common ground based on their clients' wishes, a temporary compromise was reached on separating our assets. I received the Carrollton house and the expenses related to it, and Frank was responsible for the luxurious house in California and the condo at Lake Tahoe. Frank and I each received half of the funds remaining after deducting the expensive attorneys' fees. The judge also froze the amount that Frank's lawyers could withdraw without the court's approval.

As with the bail hearing, this court hearing was widely covered by the media. Television cameras seemed to be everywhere, with eager reporters seeking comments from anyone they could accost. The hearing lasted the entire day, as did the media coverage. As we were leaving the courthouse, the attorneys made a short statement and then asked if I wanted to speak. I did. Remembering all those prayers that had sustained me during the long hours in ICU and in rehab and the promises I had made to the Lord, I began to say what was on my heart: "During and after the shooting, I continued to pray, thanking God to be alive, for being with me, and for saving me from death." The media reported my entire statement on the evening news. When it was picked up by the national media, I received numerous calls from various TV producers, but I wasn't yet ready for that kind of attention.

My body was beginning to heal, as much as it ever could, but I continued to deal with the emotional trauma. Because I could now wear my own clothes, I needed to accompany my brother to my house to get more of my things. With each trip, my brother and mother encouraged me to stay a little longer, but I still could not force myself to go into the garage. My trauma counselor gave me some exercises to help me over that hurdle. My mom would drive me to the house and park in the front. Then I would begin walking along the side of the house. As I approached the driveway, my heart would begin to race, and by the time I reached the driveway, my whole body would be pounding with fear. I would wait for a few minutes, praying for God's peace, until my anxiety subsided. Then I was to open the garage door and look inside. Finally, I would close the garage door and walk around in the driveway and alley, just breathing deeply to gear up for another look.

I repeated this exercise over and over for the next twenty to thirty minutes, or until my body and mind were calm enough for me to walk halfway into the garage. The final hurdle was going all the way into the garage where I had faced my attacker and looked down the barrel of his gun. I would stand in that location until I began hyperventilating and had to run from the garage. The process was exhausting but necessary. I had to face, fight, and destroy the demon of that nightmare. Like my physical recovery, my emotional healing took place in baby steps.

Another major step in my recovery was returning to my church. That was a place where I knew I was loved and where I gained so much strength. At the end of September, my daughter, son-in-law, and mother went with me to a Sunday service. We deliberately went late and sat at the back of the auditorium. At the end of the service, my pastor announced that a very special person was in the congregation. Before I knew it, I was surrounded by my Christian brothers and sisters, all anxious to see for themselves how I had survived. So many hugs and pats on my shoulder that were meant as expressions of love felt like baseball bats. The extensive nerve damage to my arm and back made even the slightest touch excruciatingly painful. Unless one has had that kind of nerve damage, it's hard to understand that "even the weight of a dime causes pain," as one of my doctors had explained. I was wearing a sling to remind my friends not to hug or touch that part of my body. Sometimes it helped, but not enough.

In mid-October, I met with the doctor who was to create my prosthetic eye. This was the first in a series of visits at which the doctor stretched my eye socket so that the muscles would hold the prosthetic in place. The process was incredibly painful; it involved inserting a plastic mold to hold my eyelid partially open until the next visit. At this point, I removed the patches that I had been using to cover my eye, patches that my sister-in-law had decorated to match whatever I was wearing.

After about a month, I went in to get my prosthetic eye. The doctor spent most of the day making the eye, a tedious process that involved matching the color to my natural eye, then adjusting and readjusting the fit. I was amazed at his skill, his artistry with color, shape, and size. The result was stunning. However, he told me that I would need several more prosthetics before the final one. Because the prosthetic sat a bit lower than did my natural eye, I would also need further surgery to rebuild the "orbital floor" that had been destroyed by the bullet. But that surgery would have to wait for further healing.

CHAPTER 7

Beginnings and Endings

During the many weeks of physical healing, I had days of joy that helped to distract me from my losses. Church friends persuaded me to go along on a mission trip to Florida to work with women in faith-based shelters. Becoming involved in the lives of these homeless women, often victims of abuse, reminded me of the blessings I still enjoyed, the blessings of my Lord and the support system I had of fellow believers. One of the strongest of my fellow believers, my brother, is a pastor in Driftwood, Texas. At his church, I gave the first public testimony of my horrific experience and God's power that had enabled me to survive. To add to my joy, I sang in a quartet with my brother and two high school friends, the song "The King Is Coming."

To resume a more normal life, I realized I needed to find a place to live. Although all the traces of the crime had long been removed from the house by a hazmat crew, I still resisted the idea of living there. I began looking at smaller places, especially several new condos in a convenient area. But as the Christmas season approached, I found myself becoming more and more drawn back to the home that Frank and I had built together. I remembered several verses that God had impressed upon me during that time, one of which was in Zechariah: "'Not by might nor by power, but by my Spirit,' says the LORD Almighty." I experienced the Lord's assurance that He would protect me and that I should return to my own home.

Mom and I began packing up our cars with my belongings, and we moved back into the house. I was home at last, and not just physically. The enemy—the terror from that night—had finally been defeated. God had given me victory. Although Mom slept with me for the first few nights, I was soon strong enough to sleep alone. I needed to recover a sense of normalcy—"the new normal," as people sometimes say.

Although I wasn't yet ready to go into the garage, I did feel safe enough to walk out the front door to the mailbox. As I began fumbling through a stack of mail—advertising circulars, credit card applications, cards and letters from friends—one letter caught my eye. The handwriting was messy, and the envelope was soiled. It was addressed to "John Howard," and it bore a prison return address with an inmate's name: Billie Earl Johnson.

My heart started racing. I felt clammy and lightheaded. Was Billie lurking around the house to see whether his letter had arrived? After all, he obviously knew where I lived. But no, the letter had come from prison, so he must be there. Clutching the edge of the letter with two fingers, I raced into the house and double-locked the front door. *What to do?* I told myself that the letter might be evidence, so I should try not to leave my fingerprints on the envelope. I picked up the phone to call for the police—a flashback to that previous call. Luckily, an officer soon arrived to take the letter, still unopened. A few hours later, the police detective called to read me the letter. I almost had to laugh—he was begging Frank to bail him out of jail.

As I became more comfortable at home, I determined to celebrate Christmas by putting up a small tree that used to decorate a guest bathroom. With each ornament that I uncovered in the box of decorations, memories of past Christmases reminded me of happy times. Frank and I had usually bought an ornament in each place where we had traveled. As I looked through the ornaments, my eye went immediately to the first one we had ever bought together—while on our honeymoon in Hawaii.

The contrast between our previous Christmases and this one was stark. Instead of Frank, the children, and me celebrating together, this year we were all scattered. Our older daughter and her husband were in California, where their jobs had required them to move, and Frank was still restricted from any contact with me. That left only my son and his wife, our younger daughter, and me to celebrate the holiday, and not in our house but in my son's apartment. But in that year, 2012, we began a new tradition: Each of us painted a Christmas ornament depicting one of the names of God, and writing a message telling why that name was special to us.

With the new year came continued sessions of physical therapy on my right arm, as well as massage therapy twice a week. Although all this treatment was agonizingly painful, my use of that arm was improving. However, my prosthetic eye was becoming troublesome—a problem that I could find laughable. I remembered past occasions of crawling around on the floor to find a friend's lost contact. Now I found myself crawling around to find my eye, which was frequently popping out—easier to find than a contact lens but much creepier. I entertained myself by writing this account of my errant eye:

When my sleep alarm (not my burglar alarm!) went off this morning, I popped out of bed ready to go, and marched into the bathroom ready to start my shower. But when I went to the sink and looked in the mirror, what did I see? ... I was back to only one blue eye! Somehow my prosthetic eye had fallen out in the middle of the night! So, I promptly went back to my bed and began to search for a stray eyeball—and there it was, staring right back at me!

So, I went back to the mirror and worked a bit to put it back in and finally was successful. However, there must be a trick I missed out on...because when I got in the shower and was washing my hair, suddenly out of the "blue," my eye shot out like a speeding bullet. (That "speeding bullet" phrase seems to be a theme in my life these days!) There it lay, staring again, right back at me!

I, along with my "wandering eye," returned to the doctor, who said that my eye socket had loosened up a bit. However, he would prefer to postpone creating a new eye until after the surgery on the orbital floor of my eye. But in the following days, when my eye continued to fall out, he decided to make a new eye before the surgery was to take place.

Even though these physical difficulties were consuming much of my time and efforts, the financial and legal issues still had to be resolved—issues mostly related to the question of whether to finalize the divorce. I sought counsel from my attorney, as well as from an associate pastor who was also a close friend. On the one hand, my children feared that a divorce before the trial would be detrimental to Frank's case. And then there were also the marriage vows I had made to Frank and to the Lord.

I thought back to the promises we'd made even before we married. As strong Christians, we agreed that God would be the true head of our household, and that we would pray for His direction on any decisions we needed to make. Although I worked for the first few years of our marriage, Frank wanted me to stay at home when our children started school, so that I could participate more fully in their activities. We both were committed to raising our children to know the Lord and to represent Him well. We attended parenting classes and shared in our kids' interests—sports of all kinds, theater, and music. Raising our children was priority number one, and respect for their dad was a top priority for me.

For several days, I agonized over whether to divorce the father they adored. Would the loss of my marriage cause the loss of my children? An even stronger pull was my realization that I still loved him, this man with whom I had shared so much of my life. *That* man was the one I knew and loved, not this stranger who was reported to have wanted me dead. I prayed for God's guidance and for the strength to follow His will. But the stark reality of my situation was that only a divorce could protect my financial health—both now and in the future.

And so, I called each of the children to let them know I was moving forward on the divorce. Although I had always avoided ever criticizing Frank in front of our children, I had to be completely honest with them at this point. The disaster that had come to our family was the result of Frank's own bad decisions. I wasn't out for vengeance against Frank, and I would never deliberately do anything to jeopardize his case, but I also had to take responsibility for myself and my financial circumstances. The children were ambivalent about my decision. Logically they understood my dilemma, but emotionally they grieved. And so did I.

My attorney notified Frank through his attorney that I was moving forward to finalize the divorce, a message that generated the usual flurry of attorney-guided negotiations. As usual, Frank's attorney wanted to revisit several financial decisions that had been made in an earlier agreement. The most surprising request, however, was Frank's—for the two of us to try reconciliation counseling before finalizing the divorce. At first, I was astonished by the suggestion, but then I began to suspect that his request was probably a ploy to delay the divorce until after the trial.

CHAPTER 8

Celebrations and Sadness

The decision to finalize the divorce marked a new phase in my life—ironically appropriate, because my birthday in February was approaching. A few days before my birthday, I had the opportunity to speak at my oldest brother's church and to feel the love and support from that congregation. The church service was followed by lunch at my brother and sister-in-law's house, as well as an inspiring conversation with his ninety-year-old pastor. Sitting out on the patio with family and friends while my brother grilled burgers, I felt at peace. After that, I celebrated my actual birthday by having lunch with Mom and dinner with another brother and his wife. To remind myself of this happy day, I posted this message on Facebook:

> With a grateful heart, today, February 19, 2013, I get to celebrate my fifty-second birthday. On August 18, 2012, what Satan meant for evil, God—the one true God, my heavenly Father, and Jesus, my Savior and Lord—turned for good and saved my life from a speeding bullet. I praise God for all He has done in my life, and I thank each of you, my family and friends, for your many prayers, encouragement, cards, calls, gifts, and service that have helped me in my recovery. I still have a lot of recovery ahead, but I know that God will continue to see me through.
>
> Isaiah 41:10 says, "I have chosen you and have not rejected you. So do not fear, for I am with you; do not be dismayed, for I am your God. I will strengthen you and help you; I will uphold you with my righteous right hand."

Ever since the shooting, I had thought about my 911 call for help and the police dispatcher who had been my angel during those first terrifying minutes. So, I called the detective for an appointment to hear the recording that had been made. Listening to that call, made on August 18, I was transported back to the garage and to the gun pointed at my head. I was shocked at the sound of my voice—so weak, barely audible, choking (I remembered) on blood—and I was amazed at the calm and kind voice of the dispatcher, Dustie. The call lasted about five minutes—five minutes of a nightmare relived. Again came the tears, along with the pain of lost love, lost health, lost security. Healing was yet to come.

And yet, I still experienced joy at the reminder of God's faithfulness through those dark days. He had truly rescued me "from the pit."

During my conversation with the detective on that day, I mentioned how much I owed to the dispatcher for helping me through those five minutes. I was excited to learn that Dustie was there, in the dispatch room, and that I could finally thank her in person. I don't know who was more thrilled—Dustie or me—me, for meeting my real, live angel; or Dustie, for having the rare delight of seeing a person whom she had helped through a crisis. I was overjoyed to learn that she had even received a commendation for her handling of my call. Later I learned that Dustie had been voted Dispatcher of the Year by the State Association of Dispatchers. At the suggestion of the Carrollton Police Department, I was invited to attend the awards banquet to present Dustie with her award. It was the first time a victim had ever been invited to present the award.

At the time they asked me to make this commitment, they didn't have a firm date for the event, but I accepted the invitation contingent on the date of my next eye surgery. As it turned out, the date was May 21—the very day I would have been celebrating my thirtieth anniversary with Frank. Another irony. But the experience of honoring Dustie was such a blessing that it dwarfed any bitterness I might have otherwise felt on that date.

When I presented the award, I prayed for all the 911 dispatchers, and I thanked Dustie for "being the instrument God used to comfort me while I waited for help to come." I told her that her "confidence, knowledge and listening ear were perfectly balanced" with her "compassion and willingness to meet my need at such a fearful time." It was a joyful celebration of the role Dustie had played in saving my life and of my gratitude to her for being God's angel to me.

Not only did I have the opportunity to speak of God's power in saving my life, but my mom and I were treated to an all-expense-paid trip to Houston with accommodations in a very nice hotel and a delicious dinner. I was overwhelmed by the special treatment I received, and I was grateful for the distraction that it provided. Instead of dwelling on thirty years of marriage and the upcoming divorce that would mark its final demise, God had blessed me with the chance to show my gratitude to Him and to His angel, Dustie. A thankful heart is a happy heart!

A setback in my emotional healing, however, soon came through a message from my attorney. Frank's attorney had proposed a division of "community assets" that indicated his unwillingness to provide me with any maintenance income. This refusal felt like another bullet—but this time to my heart. As I had asked myself so many times before, I again wondered what I had done to make Frank hate me so much. I yearned to ask him why he had veered onto this path that was now destroying our family. But the restraining order that kept him from any contact with me also prevented such a conversation; perhaps it was God's way of protecting me from further hurt.

Because of our inability to agree on a property settlement, my attorneys and I met with a mediator, who then met with Frank and his attorneys. These meetings lasted late into the night, but after a grueling day, we finally reached an agreement. Although I could have pressed for a greater number of assets, many of them were tied to Frank's gifts to his mistress, and I wasn't prepared to endure the lawsuits that would likely result from further demands. It was time to end the wrangling, at least for the time being.

One of the issues in the settlement was related to Frank's CPA license, which was in danger of being revoked. I remembered how we had both made sacrifices for him to earn it, first by cutting our honeymoon short to enable him to finish the requirements for his college degree. Then there were those many months of study in which he prepared for the licensing exam. And now that very license was in jeopardy because of Frank's behavior. I guessed that, because it represented our partnership together, I simply couldn't bear for it to be lost. I also knew how detrimental it would be for Frank to lose his license, and I had promised our children that I would try to avoid hurting their father. Hiring an attorney to fight the revocation was expensive, but I decided to pay for it, contrary to my attorney's advice. I had to limit the damage to our lives as much as possible. And if Frank was acquitted, he would need that license.

My journey toward physical healing took a step forward when I met with the eye surgeon who would rebuild the orbital floor for my prosthetic eye. After determining that sufficient healing had occurred, the doctor scheduled the surgery for the end of March: seven and a half months after the shooting. I received even more good news when I met with the doctor from the rehab hospital. He was amazed at the progress I had made in the therapy on my arm and hand. His initial comment was "Wow!" He had not anticipated that my therapy would be so successful due to the extent of my injuries. Had he known, he said he would have video-recorded my progress to show to his medical students.

With all this physical healing taking place, I was becoming aware of some cognitive problems. I had been told at Parkland that I had sustained slight brain damage from the bullet, but I had hoped it would not be noticeable enough to bother me. But I began having trouble processing information I would hear and would need to have it repeated. Several tests revealed a problem in the auditory area of my brain. So…more therapy—this time twelve weeks of brain-stimulating exercises, especially exercises to improve my attention span. The good news was that my hearing was not actually impaired.

CHAPTER 9

Division and Unity

There was no good news on March 21, 2013. After hearing the prosecutor's case against Frank, the grand jury chose to indict him on six counts of criminal solicitation, one count of attempt to commit capital murder, and one count of conspiracy to commit capital murder. He was given several days in which to turn himself in, which would then be followed by another bail hearing. Our children and our entire family—including me—were stunned by this sobering news. Emotions ranged from disbelief, to relief, to hope for the evidence needed to exonerate him. As the prosecutor enumerated the indictments, one after another, I felt as though my heart was about to explode. The tears came in torrents—a profound grief for the man with whom I was still in love, a man who had everything but had thrown it all away.

With the indictments, the evidence against Frank became a matter of public record. Up to this point, I hadn't been allowed to tell anyone about the evidence that the police had shared with me. But it was now time for our children to learn some of the details of the case against Frank. I told them about the text message that Frank had sent to one of the hired killers a few minutes after the shooting: It was one simple word—"status?" Most chilling was the alleged conversation in which Frank suggested the hit take place at the Gaylord Texas Hotel, where I was attending a conference, and his instruction that a knife or bat be used because a gun would cause too much commotion. The children, especially our older daughter, were still adamant that the allegations would be disproved at the trial, scheduled for August.

I had little time for reflection before I began getting calls from various media outlets wanting interviews. I decided to accept one request from a local television station to produce a video. After running part of the video one night, the station received such a large response that they aired more of it the next night. The interviewer, Rebecca Lopez, was incorporating my story into an ongoing report about abused women. The day after the video aired, she received a call from a woman who had become so inspired by my story that she made peace with her estranged sister.

Public knowledge about the indictment led to a barrage of interest from national media sources, especially news programs like *Dateline* and *48 Hours* that wanted to interview me. My immediate response was to refuse their requests, but then I realized I had not prayed about that decision. When I asked the Lord for His will, He directed me to Jeremiah 1:7–8, a passage in which God tells Jeremiah not to be afraid and to go to "everyone I send you to and say whatever I command you." I considered those verses to be my answer and contacted the representative from *Dateline*.

The interview process with *Dateline* took place over several months in Carrollton, followed by taped interviews in New York with my two daughters. In their interviews, they defended their father by claiming that he had been framed and would ultimately be exonerated. I understood their loyalty to their father, but I wished it had not come at my expense. Even if Frank was innocent, I was still a victim who had suffered greatly because of his bad choices. Nevertheless, I was generally pleased with *Dateline's* handling of the story, which aired the year after Frank's trial.

About this time, I needed a respite from the turmoil in my family so that I could focus on the eye surgery scheduled for the week after the indictments. This surgery to rebuild the orbital floor was necessary to support the prosthetic eye. Although I arrived with my mother and my brother at 6:00 a.m., the surgery was delayed until 3:30 p.m. because of several other medical emergencies the doctors had to tend to. It was a long wait, but we tried to remain patient, remembering that I had recently been the emergency that had, in turn, probably delayed other scheduled surgeries. My surgery lasted three hours, longer than expected because the damage was more extensive than expected. The surgeons had trouble finding enough structure left to attach titanium plates to hold the eye in place.

The first few days after surgery, the pain level was much greater than I had expected. Because I needed so much medication, I remember little of that period. Mostly I went from sleep to a semiconscious state and then back to sleep. But on Easter morning, four days later, I was alert enough to realize I wouldn't be attending church that day. I was still too weak even to get dressed, so I was grateful to be able to worship with my church family by watching the service online. Celebrating Christ's resurrection that Easter was especially meaningful to me, for I was beginning to experience the resurrection of my own life.

I was further encouraged the following week when I received a good report concerning the surgery. I was healing well and would likely be ready for the new prosthetic eye in just another month. In the meantime, I decided to wear my decorative eyepatches again, to hide the "Frankenstein" appearance that had been created by the surgical stiches.

The physical progress I was making didn't carry over into the emotional healing I needed. Now that the evidence against Frank had become public and I had shared some of it with the children, they had so many questions. Frequently our older daughter would ask me to clarify certain pieces of evidence against her dad. Because she loved and respected him so much, she was now on a crusade to disprove the allegations. Even though I understood her motivation, her frequent questions to me were taking a serious toll on my emotional health. I was still weak from the surgery and was easily exhausted by frequent calls, not only from her, but also from financial and insurance institutions and attorneys—especially Frank's divorce attorney.

As these aggravations increased, my emotional and spiritual strength declined—to the point that I began to grow more and more angry. Small irritations seemed magnified. I was annoyed by the sound of my mother's voice. (Only my precious dog could soothe me.) I was angry at the children for their lack of compassion for what I had been through. I was angry at Frank for all his bad choices and for associating with the lowlifes who were connected to my shooting. Whether he had gotten involved with them because of bad business deals (as he claimed), or he had hired them to kill me, he was responsible for the bullet that had changed everything. I must admit—I was even angry with God for allowing this disaster to happen to me. That anger led me to spend many hours talking with God and praying for deliverance from that destructive emotion, a prayer that He answered

I knew then, as I know now, that God can handle my anger, but I also realized that I myself couldn't. Again, He reminded me of His love and compassion. Although my anger diminished in the following months, I would still have times when I struggled greatly with it.

A respite from my anger came unexpectedly through our younger daughter's college graduation. She was adamant about wanting both Frank and me to come to Nashville for the ceremony. Because Frank was not allowed to travel across state lines or to be around me, I had the dilemma of either disappointing her or legally requesting a waiver of the restraining order. I decided that this milestone in our daughter's life was a priority, especially because I suspected an engagement to her long-time boyfriend would likely be a part of the celebration. Still, I was torn, halfway hoping that the judge would deny my request. But he didn't.

Graduation weekend was not the disaster I had feared. Our daughter got to spend time with both Frank and me—but not together. He opted to skip the graduation party because he realized that his attendance would make me uncomfortable, as indeed it would. Although I believed this magnanimous gesture was primarily an *act* to impress the children, I was still relieved to be spared from being in his presence.

The weekend was made even busier by our daughter's move into a new apartment. I had decided to give her several pieces of furniture, which Frank then brought to Nashville. That necessitated packing and unpacking items for the move. Our daughter's "intended" also met with Frank and me separately to ask for our blessing on their proposed marriage, one request that was easy to grant.

To add to the festivities, it was also the weekend before Mother's Day. I was thrilled when both of my daughters presented me with sweet cards and scrapbook pages detailing important events in their lives during that year. (Scrapbooking was a hobby the three of us had shared.) Thus, the weekend became a joyous interlude, a welcome break from the grief we had all been suffering. It was also a gift from God to comfort me with the knowledge that He had forgiven me for my anger toward Him.

In some ways, this Mother's Day following my daughter's graduation weekend felt like the beginning of my "new normal." As another new "first," I celebrated the day in church—but this time alone. All three children called, each with sweet expressions of thanks to me. But our interactions were changing. I was no longer the dutiful mother and indefatigable cheerleader for their dad. The evidence I had received from the detectives had begun to convince me that Frank had, indeed, hired someone to kill me. I couldn't pretend otherwise, not even with the children.

A significant chapter in this "new normal" came with the awareness that I needed to sell our house as soon as the divorce was final. The next weeks were consumed by the dual tasks of working with a realtor friend from church to find a new place to live and the onerous work of preparing to move. With many decisions to be made, I was thankful that the nerve pain in my right arm had diminished quite a bit so that I could reduce my pain medication and think more clearly. Deciding what to keep and what to give or throw away consumed many hours during this time. The children helped when they could. In fact, we spent many hours laughing at old pictures, trophies of forgotten awards, stuffed animals, school essays—all the artifacts of happier days. Occasionally Frank's help was needed, necessitating my leaving the house so as not to be near him.

Days of packing and searching for a new home were punctuated by various doctors' appointments. A visit to my nerve specialist provided me with another step forward in my healing. The good news—no further surgery was needed, and I was *released*! That word had taken on new meaning in my life. And then my prosthetic eye doctor informed me of still more progress. I had healed sufficiently from the last eye surgery for him to begin work on my new eye. He put another stretcher in my eye socket so that it would be ready for the prosthetic within the next few weeks.

CHAPTER 10

New Home, New Life

A conversation with a close friend made me realize that I was also healing emotionally. Because she had been with me from the beginning, she reminded me of instances of PTSD that I had exhibited. On one occasion, I was so afraid of going into her garage that I insisted on remaining in the hallway while she opened the garage door to back out her car. I even wanted to wait inside the house until she closed the garage door. And then there was the progressive dinner we attended together. She asked me whether I remembered locking the door immediately after entering the home of one of our hostesses. I didn't and was glad.

A major milestone in my healing would come when I found a new home. With the finalization of the divorce—which was fast approaching—I could now sell the house, so my realtor and I stepped up the search for my next home. For several weeks, the search was a journey in highs and lows, as one possibility after another was thwarted. Along with the house-hunting came the seemingly endless work of preparing to sell the house in which I had lived for many years. Although I had many friends to help, the responsibility of selling and buying a house was new for me. In some ways, it was like learning a foreign language, but I was determined to rise to the occasion. After all, I had learned countless medical-related facts—facts about my body, surgical procedures and specialties, and types of injuries. I was earning a degree in Changing One's Life.

With the finalization of the divorce, I completed the greatest requirement for that degree. It had been preceded with many tears. In a session with my trauma counselor, I described the happy anticipation Frank had expressed about our someday becoming "empty-nesters." He had even asked that I not work so that we could travel together and enjoy being just a couple again. But the love of my life had abandoned me, and with that loss came the loss of the identity I had had for the last thirty years. What I did have left was the belief that God takes what is meant for evil and turns it into good. I hung on to that comfort.

I wondered how long I had to wait for that good to come, ultimately realizing that the good would come only through very small steps that I needed to take. I had to find joy in the most mundane of blessings—finishing packing up all up the kitchen items I wanted to keep, disposing of boxes of memorabilia that the children didn't want, looking at potential new homes for myself. With each task completed, I was moving forward, ever so slowly. And finally came the day the divorce was finalized. On June 24, just as I was finishing my morning devotional and prayer time, my attorney called with the news. Another hurdle cleared, but one that gave me little joy.

With the divorce behind me, I needed to step up my pace in preparing to move. The house I had thought was perfect for me had come back on the market after having had two contracts fall through. That news motivated my realtor and me to move more quickly in getting my house on the market. With that task accomplished, I was free to visit my younger daughter to help plan her wedding. While I was there, my realtor called with news that she had found an even better property for me, but because several other buyers were interested, we needed to move quickly. As soon as I returned and saw the place, we made an offer. It was at that point that I saw the Lord taking over. I had done my part, and now I saw Him bringing about the amazing results: the buyers of my house closing on the house they were leaving; the next day the buyers and me closing on my house; and later that same day, closing on my new house.

When I finally got moved in to the new place, with much help from one of my brothers and his son, I felt my new life had finally begun. Unpacking boxes, finding places to put that end table, that picture, that set of dishes—such tasks, though sometimes difficult physically, helped me to adjust to this new reality. More help came from my uncle, who assembled my new kitchen table. And as soon as I could start decorating, I was once again in my element. Having to leave the home that I had poured so much effort and creativity into was very difficult, but now I could start all over, with a new challenge. I needed that.

This challenge was a new adventure for me, since I had never lived completely alone and on my own before. I had married Frank and moved out of my parents' home into our home. For the first time in my life I would be decorating for me, with female only considerations. While I had to be careful in my spending, that was a happy time as I enjoyed looking for new colors and décor for my home. After a few weeks, friends who were excited for me would say, "I can't wait to see your 'new pad,'" or "your 'new place.'" When they said this, I would think to myself, *It's not a "pad" or a "place"; it's my home.*

That thought prompted me to pray for a name to call my new home. I considered how the Bible records God's instruction to His people to "build an altar" and give it a name, to memorialize God's revealing Himself or commemorate a miracle that took place in that location. I chose "Grace Cottage" as the name—*grace*, because that is the meaning of both my first and middle names, but more importantly, because it is only by God's grace that I am even alive. And *cottage* is an acronym that was inspired by a verse that I had read the morning of the shooting: "The LORD your God is with you; he is mighty to save. He will take great delight in you; he will quiet you with his love; he will rejoice over you with singing." Anyone who comes to my home sees this acronym on a wall hanging by my front door:

Christ's conquering

Over

Trials and temptations

Trusting

All-sufficient

God- given grace

Exuberantly

The verse that inspired me, Zephaniah 3:17, became significant in my healing. God would bring it to my mind, always at the right time, through a text from an out-of-state friend or a sermon on the radio. The Grace Cottage name/acronym was painted on a canvas in my new design colors by one of my sweet and talented friends. This canvas is a reminder of the journey that led to the home of Nancy Howard, a survivor and a divorced empty-nester.

With my new home came the realization that I needed a job to supplement the income that I had been awarded in the divorce. But what to do? I hadn't worked full-time outside the home since the early years of my marriage. I was a homemaker, a mother, and a wife. Once again, God provided what I needed: a job that suited my physical limitations but also one that I was perfectly qualified to do. A couple in my church who both worked needed after-school help for their children. They needed *me*. So, I began picking their children up every afternoon and staying with them until their parents came home. The extra income was a blessing, and the love I developed for these children and their parents, another blessing.

But along with the godsend of this part-time job came unhappy news when I went for a checkup with my eye doctor. He said that I would need yet another surgery to support the prosthetic eye properly. My eyelid had been so damaged that all that remained on the inside of it was scar tissue. To correct the problem, he would need to take some tissue from a cadaver and graft it to my eyelid. Learning that I was facing more surgery coincided with the district attorney's work to prepare me for Frank's trial. That preparation involved many hours in which I heard again the disturbing evidence that witnesses would be revealing. In some ways, that was a trial for me, for the trial to come. I needed strength to deal with all the ugliness in our lives that would be exposed to the world. I poured out my heart to God:

> *Lord, I praise You that Your love, mercy, and grace go far beyond salvation. I have been in such emotional, mental, and psychological pain trying to walk through this valley of the shadow of death—the death of my life and dreams as I knew them on August 18, 2012. I am lonely, excruciatingly lonely. The graduations and birthday celebrations are over, and my son and daughter-in-law have left for California, not to visit but to live. My real life has now begun…living alone.*

> *Father, with a broken heart over the brokenness in my life, I ask You to change my heart. During the last month, my anger over this tragedy has consumed me. It's an ugly, ugly dark hell, this anger. God, living right now seems like death—not just "the valley of the shadow of death." But You know that. You're here walking with me through it. You share this pain, this cutting to the soul. I hate this life, yet as I scream it in my soul, You know my thoughts and understand, but still You walk with me.*

> *Lord, I give You my hurts: deep, deep grief; anger; bitterness. Lord, I sense in my spirit that it's time for me to write down what I've finally come to believe in my heart—I believe Frank did make those plans to kill me. Even though he is the father of my children and I don't want my children to be hurt, I believe that he should go to prison. With mourning—deep in my soul, Father—I release him to You and ask that You provide Your justice.*

> *I sense Your holy presence—Your healing, comforting balm, and Your peace that passes all understanding, enfolding me like a garment…a garment of righteousness. Isaiah 61:10 reminds me to "rejoice in my God, for He has clothed me with garments of salvation and arrayed me in a robe of righteousness." I praise You, Lord God! I'm free to embrace the new life You have planned for me.* **I praise You for doing the work only You can do. Thank You, Lord, for loving me and staying with me through this valley of death.**

CHAPTER 11

Called to the Stand

August 5, 2014: After several postponements, Frank's trial finally begins. My emotions are all over the place. I dread what I'll be hearing, but I look forward to a resolution of the case. My mother and one of my brothers decide that each morning they will cook me a good breakfast while I have my Bible reading and prayer time. Then after breakfast, my brother will drive me up to Denton for the trial. Hearing that he plans to stay for the whole trial, I am speechless with gratitude, knowing what a sacrifice he's making. Here it is, the hottest month of the year, and he chooses to be with me every week and commute on weekends to his home and his busy air-conditioning business four hours away.

I enter the courtroom and sit behind the prosecutors. Seeing Frank at the defendant's table, along with his attorneys, I feel like a witness about to be cast between two combatants. A trial is a war, and I'm a reluctant participant.

The trial begins with the attorneys' mind-numbing recital of the exhibits—scores and scores of cell phone numbers; recordings of phone conversations; documents related to wire transfers; receipts from motels and other establishments. Then I brace for the opening statements. The prosecutor goes first. As she recounts the conversations and events that preceded the shooting, I am once again dumbfounded by their outrageous complexity. The number of players and length of time involved in the plot to kill me are astounding—and frightening. And to hear that Frank was the instigator of it all—that's the worst blow.

Testimony from first responders to the crime scene precedes my taking the witness stand. Initially, the prosecutor asks me to describe my role in the household while the children were still at home. I am grateful that this is the first question, one that I can easily answer. I describe myself as a "domestic engineer," a professional in charge of maintaining the home and caring for all of our children's needs—shopping, cleaning, cooking, chauffeuring, maintaining the family calendar to keep up with everyone's schedule (including Frank's).

I also explain my involvement in the children's many extracurricular activities in school and in church— everything from chaperoning on field trips to helping them prepare for Bible drills and sewing costumes for musicals in which they participated. When I'm asked about our family's involvement in church, I agree with my son's description: If the doors of the church were open, Frank and I would be there.

Although my primary profession was being a mom and wife, I acknowledge my employment as a part-time administrative assistant and the wedding and events coordinator at the church. The question about my hobbies is another easy one to answer. I tell of my scrapbooking, flower arranging, making cards—all the creative activities that I enjoy. Later that question becomes more pointed as I elaborate on the family calendar, noting that Frank was always aware of my activities and their locations.

The prosecutor continues with questions related to our family dynamics when the children had still lived at home. I answer that Frank and I had a very strong relationship, a great marriage though it wasn't perfect. We attended church together, sang in the choir together, and served in our youth ministry together. I emphasize the closeness of our family, how we attended events together, even encouraging our kids to go to their siblings' activities as a show of support. I also recount our hosting two foreign exchange students, from Germany and Brazil, to allow our family to extend our experience beyond our community.

Regarding the question about any marital difficulties while the kids were at home, I acknowledge a period of about four years when I had been sick with fibromyalgia and chronic fatigue. That was, I admit, a rough time for us—but it was temporary.

The questions then move to the period when Frank started working for Richard Raley. When Frank told me about his new client and the extensive traveling that the job would require, I recount an odd statement that Frank made: He hoped he would still be able to make me happy. I remember assuring Frank that I was committed to our marriage and that we would work together to adjust to his traveling. Hindsight makes me wonder whether I had inadvertently given Frank permission to move forward in his new relationship.

I continue describing the changes in Frank's behavior that began in the fall of 2009, when I returned from the mission trip to Africa. He would travel for business again and again. When he was home, he would always be invited to a hockey game or whatever sporting event was occurring. Because Frank was not a man who spent a lot of time with "the guys," it was out of character for him to attend such sporting events every time he was invited

The prosecutor later asks me if I had ever suspected that Frank was having an affair. I answer, "No, he had never given me reason to." I explain that I never felt the need to check his e-mails or text messages. Frank was a very private man, and I honored his privacy.

The subject of my direct examination turns to the discord in our marriage due to Frank's frequent absences. I'm asked whether the kids ever suspected that something was wrong. I answer that question by explaining that the kids realized I was unhappy, but I told them I was just having trouble adjusting to having an empty nest. Frank and I had always kept any disagreements between us behind closed doors and away from the kids. And because I had raised the children to respect and honor their dad, I would not complain about his absences. I would say that I was having a hard time being alone.

However, because I was acting out of character, the children thought that I was upset with them, disapproving of decisions they were making. As a result, the children and I were not getting along. I told Frank that he needed to call the kids together for a family meeting, that I would not lose my relationships with them because of our marital discord. That conversation ended in a heated exchange.

The next morning, I told Frank I wanted to talk about our fight although he probably didn't have anything to say to me. To my surprise, he said he did have something to say. He said, "I'm the right man to be the father of your children, but I'm not the right man to be your husband." I was devastated and began crying and begging Frank not to leave me. (What is too hurtful to tell the jury is Frank's response to my asking him to hold me. He not only refused, but he walked behind me, essentially turning his back on me.) I finish this part of my testimony by revealing that an emotionally charged discussion ended with Frank's finally agreeing to our trying to save our marriage.

In the courtroom, many more questions follow—questions about Frank's travel; about my hobbies, especially those that involved meetings I would attend and the locations of those meetings that Frank knew about; about changes in our income and spending levels; about bank accounts and cell phone numbers.

Then the questions begin to center around the day of the shooting and the days immediately preceding it. I summarize my activities on that day, Saturday, August 18, 2012: First, I hosted two tables at a women's tea at my church. Later that evening I attended a church service followed by the baptism of a family friend, with pictures afterwards. On the way home, I stopped to pick up dinner at a Taco Bueno and then headed home.

I'm then asked, "Where was Frank on that day?"

"He was somewhere in California with Richard Raley, who was trying to sell a car at an antique car show."

"When did Frank leave home?"

"It must have been on that Thursday because before he left, he helped me pack my car with the decorations I needed for the tea. I was planning to start decorating the next day, on Friday."

"When was he planning to return home?"

"I think he was supposed to be home on Sunday."

The prosecutor hands me an email (State's Exhibit 201) from Frank to me and asks me to read it aloud to the jury. I read it as follows:

> To: blueeyeshoward@ …….. [*I had always been known for having striking blue eyes*]
>
> *Saturday, August 18, 2012, 10:39 a.m.*
>
> *Sorry I missed you yesterday. Hope you had a good day. Also hope you had a good day today. Thanks for the devo [this was a reference to the devotions that we had tried to read together]. Really good. We didn't get everything done yesterday with Richard's car. It did not sell in the auction, so it will be in another one today. Because of all of this, I have decided to just stay over until Monday and ride back on the plane with Richard. I know that doesn't make you happy, but I think it will be the best. I know you have a busy day today so I will try to call you sometime today. I love you and can't wait to get home to you. Thank you for all you do. Frank.*

The next round of questions concerns a video that the prosecution plays (State's Exhibit 68). The video shows the parking lot of my church on August 18. According to the time stamp, the video had recorded activity in the parking lot from about 6:00 p.m. to 7:26 p.m. As I watch the video, I recognize my car in the parking lot and myself, holding an umbrella and entering the church.

The prosecutor then calls my attention to another car there in the parking lot—a car I don't recognize. As the video continues, I see myself as I'm leaving the church, getting in my car, and exiting the parking lot. The other car, which I hadn't recognize, pulls out and appears to follow me. When the prosecutor asks whether I had realized at any point that I was being followed, I said, "No, I did not." It was an eerie feeling to watch myself essentially being stalked.

The questions that follow focus on the shooting itself, the actions I took to survive, the efforts of the first responders, and the extensive medical care that I later needed—including the lengthy rehabilitation. By the end of the day, I am exhausted, both physically and emotionally, but I'm still not finished. The direct examination will continue the next day. When court adjourns, a deputy walks me and my other family members to our cars. Apparently, this is standard procedure for the protection of victims.

CHAPTER 12

Still on the Stand

Day two of my testimony begins with the 911 call that I had made. As I listen to my squeaky, almost inaudible plea, "I've been shot.... Jesus, please help me," I struggle to maintain my composure. But I also notice that I'm not alone as I see several of the jurors subtly wiping their own eyes. Another exhibit follows, my favorite shirt—beaded, purple, but now dyed brown by my blood.

Then come the questions about my surgeries—to reconstruct my face and the bone structure near my eye, and to rebuild my eyelid. I also verify that my purse, which the attacker had taken and which the police had later retrieved in a dumpster, still had cash and my credit cards inside. Nothing had been missing. I deduce that the point being made is that robbery was not the true motive for the shooting. Other questions center on my attendance at a conference at the Gaylord hotel on August 8, 2012, through August 11, as well as Frank's awareness of my intention to stay there.

Later in the questioning, I am asked whether I know a long list of different people—each of whom had a connection to Frank and/or Billie Earl Johnson. My answer is "no" in every case. I also say that I had never even heard Frank mention any of their names. I'm surprised, though, when I'm questioned about a "Marci," whom I know to have been Frank's first wife. I'm even more surprised when I'm shown State's Exhibit 164: a bank wire transfer of seventy-five thousand dollars to be sent to "Marci." The request is dated January 6, 2009, several months before Suzanne Leontieff entered the picture.

Another shock comes when I learn that Frank had even met with his first wife. I'm shown a copy of State's Exhibit 192, an admission written by Frank himself, which the prosecutor asks me to read to the jury:

> *Right after I got out of high school, I was searching for what my life would ultimately look like. I was really struggling and didn't know it. At that time, I met someone who became a good friend. She was someone I could talk to and share with. She became my best friend, my lover, and ultimately my wife. Not long after, I royally screwed up time after time. So much so that I let go of this dear friend and ran away ... for several*

years. The only thing that mattered to me . . .were the two things I threw myself into: my career and my kids.... Several days ago, I reunited with this friend. It was the most intense, passionate, painful, and at the same time wonderful experience of my life.... I don't know what this friendship will look like, but I know somehow I don't want to let it go.

These revelations about my husband of almost thirty years seem to multiply. Another exhibit in Frank's own handwriting (State's Exhibit 189) is entitled "Alliance Sales, Frank Howard's Credo." At least I know that Alliance Sales is one of Frank's clients. Yet again, I'm asked to read what he had written:

Seek first the kingdom of God. The glory of God is always the answer.

Serve others by putting their needs first.

. . . .

Give sacrificially. Time, efforts, money, et cetera.

Love your spouse. Spend time with your kids. Remember, someday they will be picking out your nursing home.

I acknowledge that, in the past, Frank had lived up to that credo in many ways, until he began the affair in 2009. I read one other exhibit to the jury that had been written by Frank (State's Exhibit 190). I don't know when he wrote it, but it reflects the Frank whom I had known before 2009:

I value my family. I strive to be the best husband and father I can be. I cherish my wife as she is my best friend. I want to be a good example to my son as to what a good husband/father should be and to my girls as to what a worthy husband should look like....

Oh, how I wish that Frank had continued living up to those lofty goals!

After a few more questions about the trips to see my mother in San Marcos, I face the defense attorney for cross-examination. He asks me to confirm that Frank has never been convicted of a crime, a confirmation I can truthfully give. Then a series of questions and answers verifying Frank's generosity to others: how he had purchased a car for my mother and for his own parents, how he gave to those in need and liberally to the church.

The questions soon begin to be more hostile, however, as I'm asked about how long I have been in counseling. Although the attorney suggests that I have been seeing a counselor for fifteen to twenty years, I correct him. I was in counseling for about four years when I was first diagnosed with fibromyalgia, starting in 1999, and again only when our marriage began to deteriorate, in 2009. At that time, I realized that a wise person would seek help when she needs it.

The defense attorney then turns to the subject of our younger daughter's wedding, which took place in early May of this year. He shows the jury pictures of the wedding, which include both Frank and me. The pictures seem to depict a normal, happy family. But then the attorney redirects a question to me about the steps I took to enable Frank to attend the wedding: writing a request to the judge to ask permission for Frank to attend, expressing my willingness to allow a picture to be taken of all of us together (if my daughter wanted one), and asking for Frank's bond restriction to be lifted for forty-eight hours so that we could be all together on that day.

When questioned about my motivation, I explain my desire to ensure that my daughter's wedding was all she dreamed it would be, and that included her father's walking her down the aisle. Denying her the fulfillment of that dream would have been unfair.

I am wanting the attorney to ask me how I had prepared for the wedding. I would testify to God's answer to my prayer for strength to help the wedding be a joyful celebration. He provided the perfect scripture passage to remind me of His presence on that day. Isaiah 61:3 was especially appropriate for the wedding's location: a beautiful garden with huge trees. The verse reads, "To comfort all who mourn, to bestow on them a crown of beauty instead of ashes, the oil of gladness instead of mourning, and a garment of praise instead of a spirit of despair. They will be called oaks of righteousness, a planting of the Lord for the display of his splendor." In order to remind myself of God's strength, which was always available to me, I found a charm with a tree on it and attached it to my watch.

Instead the defense attorney interrupts my reflections by questioning whether I had asked my older daughter to find out if Frank would dance with me at the wedding. I deny that I had done so but wish for the chance to clarify my answer. I want to explain that I was really asking whether she thought her sister would like for Frank and me to dance, just as we had done at the weddings of our two older children. Despite my discomfort in being around Frank during that time, I was willing to do anything—even dancing with Frank—to make the wedding as joyful as possible for my daughter.

The defense attorney continues his cross examination by asking a series of questions regarding one night when Frank and I went to our dance class. Although the attorney suggests that the class was only a few days before the shooting, it was really about two weeks earlier: the last day of the class took place at the end of July. Although I am unsure about the specific date, I agree that Frank and I were together for the class— and for the dinner afterward to mark the occasion.

Finally, the attorney asks when Frank had come to the hospital after the shooting. Again, I'm not sure of exactly what time, but it was the day after the shooting. I also agree that he tried to comfort me and acted very concerned about my welfare. With that acknowledgment, I am allowed to step down from the witness stand—a great relief!

CHAPTER 13

The Mistress

The next person to be questioned is, ironically, Suzanne, Frank's mistress. As she enters the courtroom, she wraps her arms around herself and utters, "Brrrrr." And when she begins speaking, I am surprised at the tone of her high-pitched voice, which reminds me of Minnie Mouse. She does not strike me as a person with much class, and certainly not the kind of woman I would have expected to attract Frank. In truth, I feel humiliated that Frank would leave me for her. I also recall my humiliation when I was first told that I should be tested for sexually transmitted diseases. Thankfully, those tests came back clear, but I couldn't help feeling dirty while watching her testify. Sin's effects are so far- reaching, contaminating everything and everyone it touches.

The prosecutor's first questions involve the circumstances of how Suzanne had met Frank, which occurred at a casino at Lake Tahoe, where they were both gambling. On that weekend in mid-July 2009, she was in Tahoe for a softball tournament, in which her two daughters were playing, and Frank was there with his friend Philip. The questions then establish how quickly their romantic relationship developed, to the point that they spent the following weekend together. Despite her living in California and Frank's residence in Texas, they continued to arrange to spend time together and to communicate often.

After numerous questions regarding cell phones and items turned over to the FBI, she admits that she had been separated from her husband and was going through a divorce. Frank also told her he was married but not happy—but that he was not miserable, either. As for the new house that Frank bought for her, paying for it in cash, Suzanne suggests a motivation for the purchase: She wanted to get away from the bad things that happened in the house that she shared with her husband.

Questions then concern trips the two of them had taken together and sporting events they had attended together, one being the trip to Dallas to attend the Super Bowl. They watched the game in Richard Raley's suite and stayed in a hotel room together. When she was in Dallas, she even visited both of Frank's offices. (I suddenly realize that as Frank's wife, I have never even seen his office in Grapevine.)

Suzanne continues describing trips that she and Frank took together, one to the Bahamas that included her girls. (This must have been the reason he came home with some new pants, an odd brand that he had never worn before, and flashier than Frank's conservative wardrobe. When I asked what in the world he was doing with pants that looked like they belonged on a teenaged surfer, he claimed they were hand-me-downs from Richard. In retrospect, I wonder if Frank was subconsciously flaunting his adulterous behavior.) Other times, Frank would join Suzanne to attend her daughters' various softball and volleyball games. As she recounts all the activities that she and Frank shared, I recognize how much of a family they had become—Frank's other family.

When asked about Frank's financial support in addition to his buying her a house, she affirms that he paid all her expenses when they traveled together. He also funded an IRA for her with five-thousand dollars, bought her a condo in Tahoe, helped with her daughter's college expenses, put her on his payroll when she lost her health insurance after her divorce, gave her a five-hundred-thousand-dollar check, bought a thirty-thousand-dollar boat for them to use, and helped with the baseball fees for one of her daughter's sports participation. Documents showing what Frank had spent on his relationship with Suzanne reveal a staggering figure: $1,926,321.85.

The next round of questions focus on the topic of divorce, specifically Suzanne's pressing Frank to divorce me. She says she first asked him about his potential divorce during their second weekend together. She describes his response to her question as to why he was not getting a divorce:

> Well, things—I mean, he was worried about [my] mental state and that she might hurt herself. And, you know, I mean, things would happen. I mean, he ended up getting cancer. I mean, his kid was getting married, graduating. So, I mean, he would—things would happen.

Her answers reinforce the effect of her voice. To me, she sounds like a bimbo. I want to look over at Frank, but don't want the videographer to catch me taking a glance. It's bad enough feeling like I'm on display. I don't want there to be a permanent record of my gazing at Frank...I don't want that additional humiliation.

The subject of our sleeping arrangement, which was raised earlier, is reintroduced when the prosecutor asks Suzanne what Frank had told her about it. She answers that Frank insisted that we were sleeping in separate bedrooms and implied that that arrangement began right after his meeting Suzanne. She further asserts that the only reason he was remaining married and living with me was not because of a marital relationship in the true sense of the word, but because of my mental instability. (So, he lied to her just as he lied to me. I guess that shouldn't be surprising.)

As she makes this statement, I can't help sneaking a glance at the defense table, and I notice Frank's reaching his hand up to rub all over his face—from his forehead down—a typical behavior pattern he follows when he is frustrated. I am amused, thinking of his likely embarrassment when Suzanne learns in front of the whole courtroom that he lied to her about our most intimate relationship.

What follows is a series of questions to Suzanne about whether she knew a list of people related to the shooting. Suzanne answers that she knew nothing about them, the same answer I have given about the same people.

Finally, Suzanne is asked about the night of the shooting. She says that she and Frank were at the condo and then went down to the casino, where she gambled and Frank stepped away to watch the Cowboys' preseason game. Shortly thereafter, Frank returned and told her that he had to leave right away.

When the defense attorney cross-examines her about that evening, Suzanne describes their efforts to find a last-minute flight for Frank to get to Dallas as soon as possible. When he failed in his attempt to get permission to use Raley's plane, he was finally able to secure a flight for early the next morning. Suzanne tells of their four-hour drive to the San Jose airport:

> We drove. Well, I drove the mountain part because he was such a mess, and then—because he hadn't heard how Nancy was, and then he found out how Nancy was and he got—we found out she was going to be okay, and he got better. And that's when I—he drove and I lost it..... I got upset.... I stayed strong until he was better.

After a few more general questions, Suzanne's testimony ends.

The prosecutor's next group of witnesses include Valerie, the ex-girlfriend of Billie Earl Johnson; Chris Johnson, Billie's brother; and Christy Johnson, Chris's wife. All three had worked at the company where Frank had worked as a CPA. These witnesses answer questions that establish the following chain of events:

- After Valerie broke up with Billie Earl, he threatened her life.

- Valerie told Chris, Christy, and Frank about Billie's threat.

- Frank asked Christy for Billie's phone number so that he could tell Billie to stop harassing Valerie.

Both Chris and Christy testify that Billie was not in any kind of business and that they never heard Frank speak of being in business with Billie. They also testify that they never again heard Frank mention Billie's name.

CHAPTER 14

Billie the Ringleader

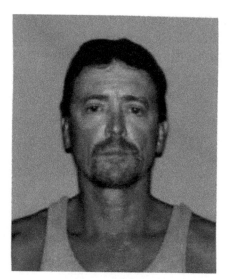

Billie Earl Johnson

The head of the Johnson clan, Billie Earl, struts into the courtroom looking like a typical thug. He is a thin man with a well-trimmed moustache and goatee, and his arms and neck are covered in tattoos. Although he's wearing an orange jump suit, an inmate's fashion statement, he seems confident as he approaches the witness stand.

The prosecutor first asks Billie about his children: Derick (his oldest), Jessica, and Kurt. Billie then confirms that he had a brief relationship with Valerie shortly after he got out of prison. When they broke up, he says he began a new relationship with Stacey Serenko right after the Fourth of July in 2009. He remembers that date because he had been in a fight on the Fourth and his ribs were still broken when they started dating.

Shortly after he got out of prison in 2009, Billie says he took a job framing houses at twenty dollars an hour, but by the beginning of 2010, he was not working anymore.

The next questions from the prosecutor involve Billie's identification of various family members and others who will later be associated directly or indirectly with the shooting:

- Molly, Billie's sister

- Ryan Rogers, Molly's son and thus Billie's nephew

- Michael Speck, also Molly's son and Billie's nephew

- Chris, Billie's brother; and Chris' wife, Christy

- Jennifer Northcutt, a friend of Billie's daughter and of Stacey Serenko

- Dustin Hiroms, Stacey's son

- Barbara Hiroms, Stacey's mother

- Jimmy Pickens, a bail bondsman

- Monte Coleman, a bail bondsman

- Robert Merrill, Billie's cousin

- John Franklin Howard, husband of Nancy Howard

After showing the jury photographs of Billie and Stacey with Frank, the prosecutor begins to question Billie about his relationship with Frank. Billie establishes the time of their initial contact as being around February 2010, when he first received a phone call from Frank. According to Billie, that was the first of hundreds of such phone calls between them, as well as around fifty face-to-face conversations.

That first conversation took place at his house in Ben Wheeler (a small town in East Texas) while Stacey was in the kitchen.

> *When the phone rang, I say "hello," and then he says "hello." I said, "Who's this?" And he says, "You don't know me, but I know you. And I don't know a lot about you, but I've heard about you." He says that he heard that I must be the one that he's looking for to do a job. And I ask him what kind of job? He said, "Kill my wife."*

> *I was laying on the couch. I raised straight up off the couch and ask him how he got this number. And he said he overheard some people talking and that they said my number and he wrote it down. He said his name was John. I asked him, "How much money have you got?" When he asked how much it would take, I said, "Bring me sixty-thousand dollars and we'll talk." And he said it would take him a couple of days. I told him to call me back when he got the money.*

Hearing those words, "Kill my wife," is so chilling to me that I feel like wrapping my arms around myself like Suzanne had done. But I restrain myself. I don't want to imitate her in any way. I furtively reach into the stash of candy that my sister-in-law had given me to have during the trial. I carefully extract a lemon drop—my stress remedy. A covered yawn allows me to discreetly pop it into my mouth.

When the prosecutor asks Billie to identify the person who made that phone call, he points to John Franklin Howard. Billie is then asked about his own reaction to the call. He answers that he talked about the call with Stacey. Then he called a friend of hers, Pat Jordan, who was a constable in Ben Wheeler. When he told Pat about the call, he just laughed it off and said to call him back if he was contacted by that person again.

Several days later, Billie was at home when John called him again. After they agreed to meet at a store in Mesquite, Texas, Billie and Stacey drove there and parked out front. As Billie walked around in the store, Stacey called him on his cell to say that she thought John was out in the parking lot. Billie then walked outside and got in the car with John Franklin Howard. Billie describes the encounter:

> He handed me a brown manila envelope that contained sixty-thousand dollars in cash and a picture of his wife and a copy of her driver's license. We made a block around Sheplers, and he dropped me back off in the parking lot of Sheplers. And I walked down the road to the convenience store, and Stacey picked me up.... I was just making sure that nobody was following us.... John said to make sure she gets killed and make it look like an accident.

To the question of what they agreed would be the next step, Billie says they just "parted ways." Only a short time later, Billie was again in jail for drug possession, after partying with all the money he had gotten from Frank. When his cousin Robert Merrill bailed Billie out, Billie called Frank to tell him that in jail "they" had taken all his money. Frank then told Billie to meet him at a Texaco station at Preston and LBJ in Dallas, the purpose being to give Billie more money. (Billie explains that the sixty thousand was just supposed to be only the first payment.) At this second meeting, Frank gave Billie an additional thirty-five thousand dollars in Citibank white envelopes, which was also a partial payment for killing his wife.

When asked what he did with the second payment, Billie replies, "I probably blowed it again. I went through it like a kid going through diapers." Billie asserts that in taking the money, he was not intending to kill me but only wanted to keep getting money from Frank. The prosecutor then asks Billie if he and Frank had discussed any ways of killing me. This is his answer:

> There was once he was talking about burning the house down, and I told him I wasn't going to do that because it could catch other houses on fire.

[We talked about] places where she would go. She was in a book club meeting. Her and her friends would go at these houses and read books. He give me the addresses and places where she was going to be. I'd go over there and take her out. Didn't make any difference if I took anybody else out as long as I got her.

When I hear Billie mention the book club, I'm reminded that the friend at whose house we "read books" had reported seeing a "peeping Tom" in the neighborhood around that time. The police had told her that closing her blinds should take care of the problem... *Hmmm...* I wonder whether the peeping Tom was Billie. Before I have time to ponder that frightening thought, Billie continues his stalking narrative:

When her and her friends was going out to town, going to the movies or go to eat, you need to make it look like a purse snatching or something. Just as long as you took her out. It didn't make any difference if her friends got caught in it or not.

As Billie is casually discussing this on the stand, I am struggling to breathe. Who is this "John" person? Where is the man I slept with for almost thirty years, whose children I carried, gave birth to, and loved? Where is the man who sat beside me in church every time the doors were opened? Who is the man who had sung in the choir with me? The man I had taught my children to love and respect? I have to fight to keep from running out of the courtroom.

Thankfully, Billie's testimony ends for the day after he says that John/Frank would sometimes use Western Union or MoneyGram to send him money, such as when his truck broke down.

Cast of Characters Linked to
Billie Earl Johnson

Chris Johnson (Billie Earl's brother, Frank Howards's co-worker)

Jessica & Derick Johnson (Billie's kids)

Jennifer Northcutt (Jessica's friend)

Charles Louderman (employed by Billie)

Michael Speck (Billie's nephew)

Michael Lorence (Speck's cellmate)

Misti Ford (Lorence's fiancé)

Stacey Serenko (Billie's girlfriend)

Barbara Hiroms (Stacey's mother)

Dustin Hiroms (Stacey's son)

Jason Rendine (Dustin's friend)

Stephanie Delacerda (Jason's wife)

CHAPTER 15

Milking John

D ay two of Billie Earl's testimony. I shudder to think what might come next. After Billie takes the stand, the prosecutor shows him copies of Western Union wire transfers from John Franklin Howard to Billie, Stacey, and Jennifer Northcutt. The dates range from March 17, 2010 to December 27, 2011. According to Billie, much of that money was used for travel expenses, including repairs to his truck and the cost of motel rooms. (Billie must be hard on his vehicles or totally inept about making his own repairs. I keep hearing about the many times he was stranded because of a faulty vehicle.)

The prosecutor also presents documentation of many larger wire transfers (up into the five figures) that were sent to both of Billie's sons, Derrick and Kurt, who had bank accounts. Because Billie didn't have a bank account himself, he would use his sons' and then give them two thousand dollars for each ten thousand he had wired to their accounts. Billie gives John's explanation for why several bank accounts were needed: to allay the concerns of John's bank about his large withdrawals.

Billie explains that he gave John's phone number to his sons so they could call him with the routing numbers for their accounts. As for the phone numbers, Billie says that John had begun using prepaid phones for their conversations.

A cousin of Billie's, Robert Merrill, also got into the action. The owner of Deep Ellum Auto Glass and Dallas Power Sports, Merrill received the same deal from Billie. In exchange for the use of his bank account, Merrill would receive two thousand for each ten thousand that Billie received from John.

Billie is asked another question about Merrill, one involving a local television interview of Billie. When the reporter had asked Billie if he had ever been in business with Merrill, Billie had answered that he had. When the prosecutor asks if that was the truth. Billie replies that he had lied when answering that question, to cover up the money transactions. Billie also denies that he and John had ever been in business together.

However, the state provides documentation for many more wire transfers from John to various bank accounts. Stacey Seneko had complained that Billie's family was getting all the money and that her family wasn't getting any. And so, Billie offered her mother, Barbara Hiroms, the same deal in exchange for the use of her bank account. Billie also admits that he had used the bank account of his daughter, Jessica, in the same way. Numerous other wire transfers of money from John to bail bondsmen (including Jimmy Pickens and Monty Coleman) and to Billie's attorney, Doug Mulder, were admitted into evidence—mostly involving Billie's many arrests.

The prosecutor then asks the question that I—and probably the jury, too— have been wanting answered: Why did Frank keep paying all this money to Billie with no results? How did Billie convince Frank that he would ever do the job? Billie describe his strategy:

> When he would call me and tell me where she was going to be at for the night, like going to the movies or something, or going to a book club meeting at Lewisville or Allen, I would drive up there, and that would give him some assurance that I was up around there.

To the prosecutor's question about who accompanied Billie on these trips to meet John, Billie rattles off multiple names—Rusty Pruitt and Jennifer Barnes, Billie's friends; Stacey; Jennifer Northcutt; Derrick and Jessica, Billie's children; Dustin Hiroms, Stacey's son; and Charles Louderman, Billie's employee and "ex-friend." (*No wonder the list of witnesses is so long!* I realize that Billie had a lot of sleazy contacts and family members.)

In response to a question about Charles, Billie describes an occasion when he gave money to "Charlie." Billie, along with Jennifer and Stacey, had met John in the underground garage at his Grapevine office. That time John handed him a red duffel bag with about eighty-five thousand dollars inside. When they went to Charlie's, Billie says he was home, and they sat together at the kitchen table:

> Charley was—like he's like six-three, six-four, big guy. And some people were trying to steal my things that I had, and so I started parking them at his house. And that's how me and him became good friends. He was watching my things.... I sat the bag on that table. And he said, "What's that?" And I said, "It's a hundred thousand dollars." And he said, "Bullshit... No, it ain't. When I opened it, he said, "Oh my God."
>
> I told him to hold it and that I would come back for it in a couple of days.... He went into his bedroom, and came out with two rifles, and put

*the rifles beside his chair and the bag underneath the chair. When I came
back, he was sitting in the same way he was when I left.*

As Billie is describing this bizarre scene, I continue to be flabbergasted that
Frank even knew a seedy character like Billie, much less conspired with
him. I can't think of a more unlikely pair to have any dealings whatsoever
with one another.

The questioning turns to the subject of Billie's brother Clifton, who died
in late 2011. To pay for the funeral, Stacey asked John for ten thousand
dollars, much of which Billie did use for funeral expenses. Billie's sister,
Molly, and her two sons—Ryan Rogers and Michael Speck—along with
their families, came over from New Mexico to attend the funeral.
Although all these relatives went back home after the funeral, by April they
returned. By this time, more people had learned about John, the "money
man." Consequently, any time Billie went to meet John to pick up money,
his kids or somebody would want to ride with him—because Billie would
always go out shopping afterward.

Testimony then focuses on prepaid phones and phone numbers, and the
number of times both John and Billie each got new prepaid phones and
new numbers. Billie admits that he would usually use the name of "Tyler
Scott" when he would purchase a new phone. (I assume that all of this discussion about changing phones is intended to show the jury the steps that
Billie and John took to cover their tracks.)

Billie also tells of receiving money from John to pay for another funeral,
for the brother of his cousin Robert Merrill, Tim. At the same time, John
also gave Billie money for a trip to San Marcos, where my mother lives.
Billie describes their conversation in this way:

> *[John] was planning to see about getting her to take a trip to her mom's
> around the first weekend of June...and I was supposed to go down there
> and take care of what he wanted took care of down there.... Kill his wife
> down there.*

The prosecutor reminds Billie of a previous trip to San Marcos, which Billie says had the same purpose: to kill me. That was the time when I had
gone to take care of my mother during her illness. Billie describes his trip
there, Stacey going along with him. Following John's directions, Billie says
at dark he left Stacey. He drove over to the house and then called John to
reassure him so the money would keep coming. When asked why he didn't
just tell John he was in San Marcos, Billie replies,

If I could have been sitting in a motel in Dallas and called and told him I'm down here and he would have asked what color of the house or where it's at, I wouldn't have no way of telling him. So I had to go get a visual of it to let him know, you know. [Billie might be immoral, but he is certainly clever.]

Before his second planned trip to San Marcos, Billie describes the occasion when he met John at a Bass Pro Shop, to pick up the money for Tim's funeral as well as cash for the next trip to San Marcos. While Billie was on his way to the store, he learned that Stacey had also invited Michael Speck, Billie's nephew, as well as Michael's wife and little boy, to come along. Billie was furious, saying "I don't need everybody up in my business!" When John finally arrived, he met Michael—a meeting that changed the entire dynamic of the conspiracy. From then on, Michael became the one to receive the money from John—but not as a messenger for Billie.

CHAPTER 16

Billie, the Felon

After that meeting, Billie was again arrested for drug possession. (How many times did this character move in and out of jail? I don't think he will ever be a candidate for a rehabilitation project.) When he called John several times from jail to ask to be bailed out, John flat-out refused. During one of those calls, which had been recorded and later entered as evidence, John told Billie, "I'm all in with Michael." Billie says he knew then that John was finished dealing with him. And Billie continues to be "stuck in jail."

As I listen to Billie's testimony, I think about the first time I heard the recording of that call, early in the investigation. I was dumbfounded by the way Frank had answered so nonchalantly, "Hey, man, what's goin' on?" Frank *knew* it was a collect call from Billie, and yet he still chose to pay for the call, *and* he'd answered it like it was from a long-lost friend! In that conversation, Frank didn't sound like a man who was being blackmailed or framed.

The prosecutor then asks Billie a series of questions about his involvement with John: Did he ever do drugs with John? Did he ever provide John with drugs, or did John ever ask him for drugs? Did he ever go into any type of business with John, other than agreeing to kill his wife? To all these questions, Billie answers, "No." And when asked whether John ever told him about having a girlfriend, he says, "Yes."

On the issue of John's growing impatience with him, Billie says that twice John asked him for a weapon so that he could just do the job himself: "He was, like—he was on a time frame, running out of time, and it had to be done this certain time or things were going to blow up or get out of whack. 'Just bring me a gun,' he said, 'and I'll do it myself.'"

My heart breaks for my children when I think about the possibility of Frank's carrying out such a vile act himself. I don't know how he will ever be able to look them in the eye again. But once again, that's why the job was delayed for so long. Frank, thankfully, couldn't go that far. Time for another lemon drop!

Billie says he talked John out of killing me himself, stating that he'd told John, "If you do that, it's going to come directly right back to you." Billie kept repeating this warning, but only because he wanted to keep the money coming. Regarding the amount he'd already received from John, Billie estimates that John had spent about a million on bail bonds and attorney fees, had given Billie about a million in cash, and had sent Billie two hundred to three hundred thousand dollars in wire transfers. When asked if he'd ever asked John where all the money came from and whether he was counterfeiting it, Billie says John laughed and said "no." Instead, he said, "I've got three bank accounts that I can draw twenty to thirty thousand—ten thousand out of each one a day."

Before the prosecutor ends his direct examination, he returns to the subject of Billie's interview with a local television station. Billie again admits that he had lied during that interview, when he said he had been in business with John and that John wasn't trying to kill his wife. When asked why he lied during that interview, Billie insists that he was trying to keep his children from being arrested, as well as trying to cover up the money transactions.

After still more questions about various phones and phone numbers, the prosecutor finally passes the witness over to the defense attorney, who then questions Billie about the time when he first heard of and then first met John. Billie continues to insist that he had never known John or even heard about John before the first phone call to solicit the murder. Billie reveals that at first, he thought it was some buddies of his "trying to play a joke or something." Regarding Billie's calling the constable, the attorney reminds him that he had been told to notify the constable if that person called again. As to the question of why he didn't make that second call to law enforcement, Billie says that sixty thousand was a lot of money.

The next series of questions and answers all reveal Billie's attempts to protect himself. He had his son Derrick take a picture of him with John. Billie also admits to having worked a deal with a Texas Ranger to stop a murder-for-hire. Furthermore, he claims that he "did a deal with the FBI and the Secret Service on counterfeit money back in the late eighties." (I can't imagine that Billie was ever on the "right" side of any law enforcement agency. If he were, he would have switched sides in a flash to make a profit.)

The defense attorney then implies in several questions the reason that Billie is testifying. Because Billie is still incarcerated for drug possession, he is just trying to get out of jail, although Billie denies that he received a deal.

When asked about his drug use and its effects on him, Billie admits using drugs, especially methamphetamine, whenever he had the money, but disagrees that it affected his memory in any way. When taken in a small amount, the drug would give him energy, but a large amount "would give you a lot of euphorium [sic]," that is, it would increase his "sexual drive."

At one point, Frank's attorney asks Billie whether he had ever taken off all his clothes and used a shotgun to blow up a motorcycle. Billie denies having been naked at the time, but admits firing at the motorcycle he had bought for Stacey because he was angry at Stacey for "taking off" on his bike.

The attorney then lists numerous felonies for which Billie had been convicted—theft, burglary of a building, burglary of a habitation, aggravated assault, and aggravated assault with a deadly weapon. The attorney's next attempt to discredit Billie's testimony focuses on whether he was receiving a reduction of his current sentence in exchange for testifying at Frank's trial. After a lengthy period of attorneys bickering back and forth, the conclusion seems to be that the state had never filed charges against Billie because he had already been convicted in federal court. Billie hoped that the federal system would give him some credit for his current testimony, but the federal prosecutor said he was cutting Billie no slack.

One of the prosecutor's final questions involves State's Exhibit 162, which is a text message that contains a picture. The text had been sent from Billie to his brother Chris, who had worked with Frank before. In the text, Billie says he is sending him a picture, and that when Chris receives it, he should let him know who the guy in the car is. Chris texts Billie back saying, "That's our CPA, Frank Howard."

The defense attorney ends his cross-examination by presenting Defense's Exhibit 16, a transcription of a conversation between Billie and an officer with the Denton County Sheriff's Department. In the conversation, the officer tries to persuade Billie to testify for the state in Frank's trial. Billie says he won't do it without a guaranteed deal. And then Billie responds by stating the obvious: "But here I sit [on the witness stand]."

I am relieved when Billie finally steps down from the witness stand. While listening to his testimony, I am astounded by how he seems to view his outrageous behavior as normal. His world could not be any more foreign to mine (or even to what I thought was Frank's world).

CHAPTER 17

Billie's Girlfriend

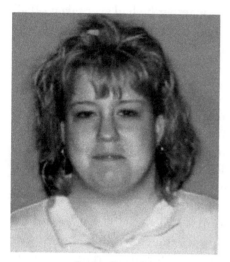

Stacey Serenko

When Stacey Serenko is sworn in, I prepare myself to hear more about Billie's unsavory world. Stacey looks as if she is fresh from the shower, her hair still damp but combed out. She is soft-spoken in her responses, and there is something hopeless about her demeanor. She reminded me of an abused dog beaten into submission but still dangerous.

The prosecutor's questions and Stacey's answers generally substantiate Billie's testimony about the first contact with Frank, known to them as John. However, in one difference, Stacey claims that she, not Billie, notified the constable about John's call. But she confirms she was with Billie when he first met with John and received sixty thousand dollars, and that she accompanied Billie to many other meetings to get money from John.

Stacey describes her life with Billie as a series of moves from place to place, from one hotel to another—doing drugs with Jessica Johnson's friend, Jennifer Northcutt; running out of money; then calling John for more—and then getting arrested and calling John to bail them out.

Regarding the time when Billie destroyed the motorcycle he had bought for her (with John's money), Stacey adds some new details:

> *I had left Billie...and he went crazy. He blew up my motorcycle. He drug his motorcycle behind the cargo trailer behind his vehicle on a logging chain down the road, down a blacktop road. He was also found on an overpass bridge in Mineola and threatening to harm himself.*

The prosecutor asks Stacey many of the same questions she had asked Billie. Although there are occasional variations in their answers, she confirms the key point in Billie's testimony: murder- for- hire as the only business that Billie had with John. Like Billie, she insists that, despite being heavy drug users, neither of them ever sold drugs. She also describes excuses they offered John for failing to carry out the hit, like missing a window of opportunity of finding me in a vulnerable location. Sometimes they would be late to catch me because their truck or car broke down; other times, Stacey says, "I might plead sickness or just stay in the restroom too long." As she lists some of their delaying tactics, I am struck by their ingenuity in keeping the money train going for two-and-a-half years.

Stacey also testifies that she would sometimes meet John in person to pick up money, often when Billie needed to be bailed out of jail. Other times John would leave money for Billie or her to pick up. When asked about those locations, she describes two: "There was a church close to where he lived that had a bus, some type of special police bus, that sat in back. And there was a dumpster, and we would pick up from the dumpster." (I'm struck by the irony—Frank, the church-going, upstanding father and husband, picks a church property to pay off a hit-man.)

Stacey also mentions another location, just as ironical. "Behind their house in the alleyway by the gas meter, we several times would pick up there." As I glance at the defense table, I notice Frank scribbling on the legal pad in front of him. I wonder if he is writing a note for his attorney or doodling, as he sometimes does when he's bored.

When asked where they followed me, she not only describes locations that Billie had mentioned but also tells about following me to an office complex. They sat waiting for me "for many hours" while I was inside, giving Billie plenty of time to slash my tires. When a friend came to pick me up, their plan to carry out the hit was thwarted because I was supposed to be stuck there for a while. I think to myself, this was probably another excuse they offered Frank. But more significantly, it's evidence that God watched over me and protected me, just as Psalms 41:11 says: "I know that you are pleased with me, for my enemy does not triumph over me."

As I mull over Stacey's account, I remember the incident clearly but had not heard it mentioned before. I wonder if Frank was surprised when I called to tell him my tire was flat and I was getting a ride home from someone at the committee meeting. I was in that office for a meeting to plan a banquet and fundraiser for a mission organization. My next thought is that this meeting was not a part of my usual schedule—Frank had to have told Billie where I was going to be! I reach for another lemon drop.

Stacey continues her testimony by admitting a falsehood. She told her mother and son, Barbara Hiroms and Dustin Hiroms, that she and Billie were getting money from John because they were business partners. The prosecutor asks Stacey a series of questions related to a business partnership:

> *Did you work at all during this time [the time they were receiving money]?*
>
> *Did you have a business during this time?*
>
> *Do you have a business plan, an investment opportunity that you were exploring?*

To all these questions, Stacey answers, "No."

> *So, what was the business?*
>
> *The business was to kill Nancy.*

Stacey finally describes John as the person I recognize as Frank. When asked how John treated her, Stacey says he was "very soft spoken, very well mannered, very—a very nice man." But when Stacey describes the meeting at Bass Pro, when Michael Speck met John (much to Billie's dismay), the "very nice man" whom Stacey had described is unrecognizable. At that meeting, John asks Billie and Michael to follow me to my mother's in San Marcos and "at whatever cost to make sure that [I] was dead. If [my] mother had to be killed as well, then...." (At hearing this, fireworks go off in my mind. Really, my mother was just collateral damage to you? She treated you like a son. I don't think lemon drops will help me now.)

Stacey testifies to the specific plans that were made:

> *June the third would have been a Monday [2012]. We were to meet with Mr. Howard and pick up a large sum of money. That was a Monday. Tuesday, we were to move the fifth wheel out of the trailer park ... and take it to East Texas and get it ready to be stored. Wednesday, we were to pick Michael Speck and drive to San Marcos, and Thursday [I] was supposed to be dead.*

When asked what "wrench" thwarted those plans, Stacey answers that she and Billie were arrested in Denton County and that they both are still in custody.

The prosecutor shows Stacey State's Exhibit 162, which is the same photograph of Frank that Billie had sent to his brother Chris. Stacey testifies that Billie's son Derrick took the picture and sent it to her phone. To the question of what she did with the photograph, Stacey says she sent it to her mother. When asked, she gives this explanation:

> *In case anything happened to me, that photograph would still make it, would still be available. My cell phone got destroyed constantly, and if anything happened, period, then that photo would at least made it through…. So [my mother] would know where to look, what to do….*

The implication of Stacey's answer is clear although the defense attorney doesn't allow her to say it: Stacey wanted documentation of Frank's involvement in the shooting in case something happened to her. Was she afraid of Frank? If Frank had really told Billie not to worry if anyone else besides me was killed, she probably should have been fearful for her own safety.

Stacey then describes actions she took to prevent the shooting, such as long rest room breaks, feigned sickness, and starting fights. As she recounts her tactics, I offer a silent prayer:

> *I praise you, Father, that you have all things under YOUR control…even people who don't know you. It has been such a vivid picture of your protection as I learn how many times you thwarted Frank's purpose, even by using Stacy Serenko, as she would cause them to be late or "miss" the appointed time. I recall a passage in Job 5 that says, "He thwarts the plans of the crafty, so that their hands achieve no success. He catches the wise in their craftiness, and the schemes of the wily are swept away." Thank you Father for revealing yourself through this situation and showing me this verse when I most needed it—to remind me of your strong arm. You held back the murderous hand until the time that YOU allowed…and then you said, you can't kill her! Wow, I'm so awed by you, my God and my shield.*

In addition to her delaying tactics, Stacey describes speaking with law enforcement personnel. In August, 2012, just days before the shooting, she was in custody in Wood County. There she told a Sergeant White about the murder conspiracy; he, in turn, contacted the FBI. When Russell, an FBI agent, interviewed her, she gave him a written statement, State's Exhibit 276, and also admitted her involvement in the case.

Even as early as October, 2010, Stacey says she spoke with Sergeant White and "another gentleman" about "what was taking place," but she didn't follow through because she got scared:

> *I didn't keep pushing.... It was such an outlandish story that people really didn't believe what was going on. I felt like at that moment when I was telling Sergeant White, that they really didn't believe the story ... I was telling them. Billie was in jail at that time, and when Billie got out of jail, I froze and didn't continue talking to the detectives.*

When the prosecutor asks Stacey whether she knew why John wanted me dead, I feel my body tense and my breathing become shallow. I want to know the answer but also fear to hear it. Stacey says John's explanation was general: "I had asked the question, is it something legal that you will get in trouble or is it more personal? Mr. Howard told me that it was a little bit of both."

I begin to wonder if the legal part of Frank's concern related to the money he embezzled from Raley. Maybe he got so tangled up in his lies that he got desperate. I want to know.

In cross-examining Stacey, the defense attorney asks why she told John she would do the job if he got her out of prison. Stacey corrects the attorney, saying she told him the "plan would go forward," not that she would do it. When asked if she was being truthful to Mr. Howard, she admits that she lied, that at that time she didn't believe that the plan would be carried out.

The defense then tries to impeach Stacey's testimony as he had tried with Billie Earl. He suggests that she is simply trying to get a reduction in her federal drug charges. She counters that insinuation saying that she tried to get help before she knew about the federal charges.

After quizzing her about her heavy drug use, the defense asks Stacey if she had told the FBI she thought maybe something else going on between John and Billie. She admits that she considered that possibility because Billie told her he had done jobs for other people that John worked for. I am surprised when the defense attorney doesn't probe further into her admission.

CHAPTER 18

Witness Parade

After Stacey is excused, two witnesses who confirm her story are called: first, James Kirk White, and next, Russell Dilisi. These are the Sergeant White and FBI Agent Russell, whom Stacey said she told about the conspiracy. Because the defense attorney doesn't cross-examine these witnesses, he must find some of Stacey's story credible, at least her assertion that she tried to prevent my death.

When Agent Russell is asked what he did with his report about the conspiracy, he says he passed it on to the Dallas office. (I wonder why the Dallas-based FBI didn't intervene. Perhaps the paperwork was delayed for a few days, too late to stop the shooting, which happened about a week later. This failure to connect the dots and prevent the shooting is a hard pill to swallow. As I listen to this testimony, the words of the prosecutor are muffled by the "if only's" that reverberate in my mind.)

The state calls Jennifer Northcutt to the stand. Jennifer is a beautiful young woman. (I am grieved that she has become embroiled in such a sordid drama at her young age.) After establishing Jennifer's meeting Billie and Stacey through Billie's daughter, Jessica, the prosecutor asks Jennifer if she ever questioned Billie about what he did for a living. She answers, "He told me he was a hit man." To the question of whether Jennifer ever saw John, she says only once, in a parking garage. She describes the incident when she went with Stacey and Billie to meet John in the garage of his Grapevine office building, where Billie got the duffle bag full of money.

To follow-up questions, Jennifer describes the first time she contacted John. It was after Billie "had kind of gone crazy," and his sons had him picked up for a mental examination. She continues by describing the situation with the motorcycles that we had heard before:

> *He blew up Stacey's motorcycle. He had her on the phone. He was trying to find her. Screaming and threatening her to tell him where she was at. He threw a brick through Jessica's windshield of her truck. He stripped down naked and got into his truck, and then took off in his truck, and went and locked himself up in my house.*

Jennifer explains that Billie had told her that if he was ever arrested she should call John to bond him out. She was able to contact John because his number was in Billie's phone, which Jennifer had. She didn't talk directly to John but just left him a message.

She continues her testimony by admitting heavy drug use with Billie and Stacey. She also confirms being with Billie when he picked up cash that John would leave for them—at a dumpster behind a church, behind his house off the alley "in a little part that was kind of squared off." On one occasion, she was present when Billie received money that John wired.

When asked about her current situation, Jennifer explains she has been serving a sentence on a federal drug charge since September 2011. Several months later, in January 2012, she told a DEA agent (Daniel Morgan), "Billie was receiving money from John to kill his wife." The prosecutor later introduces State's Exhibit 153, which Jennifer identifies as the map she had drawn for Agent Morgan. The map shows the back of our house where they picked up money from John.

Jennifer also describes conversations about how and where I could be killed. I had already heard about most of those locations, but she mentions a new one that makes the hair stand up on the back of my neck—when I would be coming out or going into the church. (Where are those lemon drops?)

The cross examination by the defense attorney focuses mainly on drug use and drug charges. His questions cast doubt on Jennifer's mental alertness due to her heavy use of methamphetamines. He also describes the federal charge of "drug possession with intent," which he insists indicates she was dealing drugs. She counters that assumption by saying that "intent to deliver" was based solely on the large number of drugs and money that she, Billie, and Stacey had.

The defense then asks Jennifer several questions about a Detective Joyce Box. Jennifer's answers confirm that Box was an investigator in Mineola that Jennifer's father had asked to delve into the activities at Jennifer's house. When Box questioned Jennifer about those activities, Jennifer didn't mention the murder-for-hire scheme. Asked why not, Jennifer says, "I was scared."

After Jennifer leaves the witness stand, the state calls Daniel Morgan, a member of the DEA task force in East Texas. Morgan confirms that he spoke with Jennifer Northcutt in January of 2012. At that meeting, Jennifer told him about the murder-for-hire conspiracy. When asked what he did with that information, Morgan says he contacted the local Texas Ranger, who inquired of other agencies about any information they had about a murder-for-hire plan or anything of that sort that involved the suspects. But no more information was forthcoming. With only the first name John, a description of him and of his vehicle, there was not enough information to launch an investigation. Furthermore, Morgan didn't know Billie's reputation at the time he met with Jennifer, although he has since learned it was bad. (I'm thinking to myself that "bad" is quite an understatement.)

During court recess for lunch, my brother and his wife and daughter join me in the victims' waiting room. Although they offer to take me to lunch, I have learned that outside the courtroom I'm likely to be recognized and even asked questions about the trial. What many people don't realize is that I am prohibited from talking about the trial since I am a witness and probably will be recalled. In fact, I can't even talk to my mother. I'm also banned from watching the news and reading newspapers. Consequently, my brother often brings me lunch, and we spend the noon time talking about other things and often praying together. I am so grateful for the sacrifice of time and travel that he and his wife are making for me.

Back in court, I'm happy as the next witness is sworn in because I know him well. He's John Hallford, the IT Director for my church. John, a former Carrollton police officer, oversees the church's computer network; is the liaison with the security personnel, including the police officers; and is responsible for the church's security system and cameras. John is the person who reviewed the church's video of the parking lot that was shown earlier during my testimony. He also provided the police a disk with all the segments of video that pertained to the case.

The day after my shooting, John studied the camera footage from the night before, Saturday, August 18, 2012. Because he knows me, John could spot my car as it entered the north parking lot, circled behind the church buildings, and parked in the south lot. He then noticed the silver vehicle that seemed to follow me and parked in the same lot.

Explaining the time stamps of the video, John establishes the exact time of each event as being synchronized with the government clock in Colorado. The video shows me entering the south door of the church at 6:00 p.m. and the silver car driving out of the parking lot a few seconds later. Then the silver car returns at 6:55 p.m. and parks in the north corner of the same lot. (John explains that the cameras are motion activated, which accounts for the time skips.) The driver then enters the south door of the church, walks to the men's rest room, and returns to the car at 6:59.

Finally, at 7:25 p.m., the video shows me walking out the south door to my car and leaving the parking lot at 7:26:40. The silver car then leaves at 7:26:45.

Although I have previously seen this footage, it still gives me a creepy feeling to see my attacker stalking me. And after hearing testimony from Billie, Stacey, and Jennifer, I know that I was being hunted many times before August 18. As John Hallford leaves the stand, I glance over at Frank, who seems to be ducking his head down to avoid looking at John, a church friend that Frank also knows very well. I wonder what Frank was thinking as he saw the video of our church, the parking lot, and the hall where he had walked so many times.

CHAPTER 19

The Parade Continues

The state's next witness is Barbara Hiroms, Stacey Serenko's mother. Unlike her daughter, Barbara has been employed for thirty years in a market as a meat cutter. Another indication that she is more responsible than her daughter is her legal adoption of Stacey's oldest child, Dustin Hiroms, when he was only three, and her having custody of Stacey's other two children. Barbara testifies that Stacey, who gave birth to Dustin when she was just sixteen, grew up in a family without much money. Stacey's father died when she was quite young.

The questioning quickly moves to the subject of money and lots of it. A few months after Stacey and Billie Earl began dating, Barbara says,

> *The times Billie and her would come around us, she would get to come to see her kids, which wasn't very often, I noticed Billie would have money, wads of money.... There were times that he would give Dustin several hundreds of dollars. At that time, Dustin was about eighteen years old.*

The prosecutor then begins to ask a series of questions to confirm that Billie used Barbara's bank account to receive large sums of money. Barbara also confirms that for each ten thousand dollars, she could keep two thousand. Then the prosecutor submits State's Exhibit 240, which lists many payments to her account, some being for as much as seventy-five-thousand dollars. One such payment, on December 14, 2010, was from one of John's companies, Snew Management, which Barbara understood to be for Billie's bail. She describes how she handled that money:

> *The money came to my account, and I was to get so many cashier checks.... It had to be given to several of the different counties where Billie ... had to pay different counties for the money that he owed.... I think one went to Rains County ... and then there was some cash money that was to be given to Stacey because one of the counties would not accept anything but cash.*

The prosecutor's exhibit shows a second seventy-five-thousand-dollar payment to Barbara's account sent from Sutaho Management Company. From that payment, Barbara says that Billie wanted ten thousand taken out in cash every day and given directly to him. When asked whether she knew what the money was for, she says, "No." Furthermore, she had never heard the name Nancy Howard.

After verifying another seventy-thousand-dollar payment, as well as multiple numbers of smaller payments—all from Snew, Sutaho, or Genschu Management Company—Barbara begins answering questions about Dustin (her grandson) and Dustin's friend Michael Speck. The last two deposits she received into her bank account were for Dustin, one being in mid-July, 2012, and the other just twelve days before the shooting.

Barbara insists that she did not know about John Howard and the purpose of the money that he was paying until Dustin became involved, which would have been as early as late May of 2012. When asked who told her, Barbara says it was Stacey and Dustin. Because Barbara admits knowing about the murder plan before it happened and before she gave money to the conspirators, the attorneys on both sides debate whether Barbara committed a criminal act and should be prosecuted. (As I listen to this debate, my heart goes out to Barbara. It appears she has walked a hard road as a widow trying to care for her three grandchildren and watching her daughter self-destruct.)

Barbara is then questioned about whether she tried to stop the murder. Answering that she did try, by talking to Jim who worked in the sheriff's department for Wood County where Stacey was incarcerated. She showed Jim the picture of John that Dustin had taken and sent to Stacey. After that, Stacey spoke with Jim about the murder plan.

As I listen to Barbara's statement, I am left wondering what this Jim person in the sheriff's department did with the information he received. Maybe a later witness will explain. I am frustrated by questions left unanswered because an attorney objects. By the time the wording of an important question is accepted, the answer often raises more questions.

The defense attorney has only a few questions for Barbara, most related to Billie Earl's bad character and reputation, which I think has already been well established.

During a pause in the proceedings, I slip a tissue out of my purse to clean the tearing around my prosthetic eye. When I notice the videographer aiming the camera at me, I quickly slip the tissue back in my purse and signal him to come toward me. I quietly explain to him that I am not crying but need to clean the tearing around my prosthetic eye. Because it's a painful process and embarrassing to do in public, I ask him not to put it on camera. I'm relieved when he graciously agrees to honor my request.

Following the brief cross examination of Barbara, Monte Coleman, Jimmy Pickens, and Pat Kinnard, respectively, are called to the stand. All three state that they are bail bondsmen who have bonded out Billie Earl as well as Stacey Serenko. Each of these witnesses also testifies to being told to contact John, Billie's CPA, for bond money and having spoken directly to John. Each is then shown various state exhibits that list cash payments or wired payments received from John for Billie's and/or Stacey's bails.

When Coleman is asked if he has ever had someone want to wire bail money into his bank account, he says, "No." In fact, that form of payment seems to have made him nervous, for once the money was in his account, he closed that account and moved the money. As he explains, someone who had his banking information to move money in could also move the money out. When asked the source of the wire transfers, Coleman reads the name that is listed in the exhibit: Sutaho. To the same question about wired payments, Pickens says his came from Snew. Neither of these witnesses was familiar with those company names.

In cross examining these three witnesses, the defense attorney focuses mainly on the criminal acts for which the bonds were posted, such as possession of a controlled substance, unlawful possession of a firearm, aggravated assault, bail jumping. As I listen to the long list of infractions for which Billie, and sometimes Stacey, needed bond money and the astonishing amounts of those bonds, I am relieved these two are still incarcerated. If they were the only witnesses who incriminated Frank, I would not trust anything they said. I wish they were the only ones, so I could discount their testimonies, so I could believe that Frank never wanted me killed.

But the prosecution's parade of witnesses seems endless. Over and over I listen to each one describe exorbitant sums of money that Frank (no, not the Frank I know—or knew) paid for criminals to get out of jail. I think about the glaciers we saw in Alaska, as they would shed chunks of ice, diminishing their mass so slowly that only over time could the cumulative loss be perceived. The testimony of all these witnesses is also cumulative, death of my faith in Frank—"by a thousand cuts."

Billie Earl's cousin Robert Merrill is asked only a few questions to confirm that he

- Never talked to John Howard on the phone or in person

- Never heard of John Howard except what he read in the news

- Never was in business with Billie

Merrill also testifies that he let Billie have money wired to one of his business accounts in exchange for Billie's paying what he owed for windshield repairs by Merrill's glass company. (I wonder if that was for Billie's daughter, whose windshield he smashed.) Billie had Merrill to give him nine thousand dollars each day until all the wired money, seventy-five thousand, was gone. The prosecutor then shows Merrill a document that lists the Genschu Management Company and the Snew Management Company as the sources for that wired money. Once again, it's clear that Frank's companies were funding his nefarious activities.

The small wooden gate between the courtroom and the testimony stand continues to swing back and forth as various witnesses come in to testify. At one point, I happen to turn around and see my sister- in-law slip in between witness to be seated in the gallery. Because of the crowd of friends and family on the prosecution's side (my side), she finds a seat only on the defense side. I'm annoyed that my "sister-in-love" can't sit close to me!

When the judge calls for a short recess and exits the courtroom, I stand up and loudly ask, "Where's my sister? I saw you come in; where are you?" She sheepishly stands up. Finally seeing her, I ask some of the media sitting a few rows behind me to please move to the other side of the courtroom so there would be room for my family. They kindly respond to my request, despite the shuffling around that it entails. My bold request surprises me, as I'm normally more reticent. But I needed "my people," especially my dear sister who keeps replenishing my stash of lemon drops and junior mints. Our reseating ends just seconds before the judge returns to the bench.

Next to testify is Billie's son Derrick Johnson, who is also accompanied by his lawyer. Derrick says he first met John Howard when Billie asked Derrick to call John to bond Billie out. At his meeting with John at a western wear company, Derrick received cash in an envelope for Billie's bail. Derrick also admits that he let his dad use his bank account to receive a wire transfer of money in exchange for a portion of it. However, Derrick asserts that he never knew why John was giving Billie money and he never heard of Nancy Howard.

There were three other times that Derrick saw John, but at those meetings he merely accompanied Billie, who talked with John while Derrick waited out of earshot. On one of those occasions, at the Bass Pro Shop in Grapevine, Derrick took a picture of John.

In cross examination, the defense attorney makes the point that Derrick has an attorney with him because he might face charges for something related to this case. He then asks why Derrick took a picture of John. To Derrick's response that he doesn't know why, the defense says that Derrick told Detective Wall that he thought Billie's meeting with John might involve drugs.

The next series of questions focuses on drugs and whether Derrick ever saw any involvement of John with drugs. Derrick answers, "No" to each question, although he gives a positive answer when asked if he ever saw Billie use drugs. A final question—did you ever hear anything about shooting a lady? A firm "No" is Derrick's answer.

Billie's other son, Kurt Johnson, briefly testifies that he allowed his dad to use his bank account to receive wired money. A state exhibit shows two wired payments came from Genschu Management Company and one from Sutaho Management Company—Frank's companies.

As Kurt is testifying, I begin thinking of the many people whose bank accounts were used to receive money from Frank. By my count, at least eight different people were getting paid directly by Frank or indirectly by Billie. I wonder why no one seemed to care enough to question the source or the purpose of all that money, just as long as they got some of it.

CHAPTER 20

Dark Comedy

One more witness to go—at least I hope so. It's been a long day already. The state calls Dustin Hiroms, Stacey's son, to the stand. He says he will be twenty-one tomorrow. (Such a young man to be mixed up in this sordid affair. I am sad that another young person likely faces a bleak future.) After some preliminary questions establishing that he lived with his grandmother, Barbara Hiroms, and that he had met John, the prosecutor begins a long series of questions regarding Dustin's involvement in the murder-for-hire conspiracy.

Dustin describes the first time he met John, on Valentine's Day in 2010. He remembers the day because he and Billie picked up some roses for Stacey before meeting John somewhere in North Dallas. The purpose, as Dustin understood, was to pick up money, but he didn't hear Billie's conversation with John. The second occasion was when Dustin went with Stacey to get money from John. Again, while Stacey spoke with John, Dustin stayed in the vehicle, a Tahoe that Stacey had bought with John's money.

The questioning moves to Dustin's association with Michael Speck (Billie's nephew), who Dustin says introduced him to methamphetamine. Dustin first met Speck in June, 2012, when Billie asked him to pick up Speck and bring him to a motel in Lewisville, Texas. A few days later Billie and Stacey were arrested and are still incarcerated. Dustin also tells of following Speck to a Bass Pro Shop in Dallas, where Speck met John and got money. At one point, Speck talked with Dustin about the hit, asking if Dustin would be the driver and he would be the shooter, a suggestion that Dustin says he turned down.

After the arrest of Billie and Stacey, Dustin says he began texting John for money in exchange for killing me. When they met at a Walmart in Terrell, Texas, John gave him a thousand dollars and discussed how the killing could occur: "Just shoot or have two crackheads run up to her and beat the sh— out of her. I mean, that's kind of brutal to say, but that's out there. I don't know how else nice to say it." (Yes, Dustin, you're right. It's brutal!)

When Dustin is asked if he offered to do that, to kill me, he says, "'Yes,' but I wasn't going to do it. I just wanted the money." He adds that he used the thousand to get high. Then a few weeks later, on July 4, 2012, Dustin met John at a Walmart in Carrollton. Dustin got in the car with John, and they drove around. Although Dustin says he was pretty much in a fog, he thinks John was showing him where he lived. The only description he can give about the house is that there was a big blue vase in the front. (My beautiful vase became a landmark for criminals.)

After John took Dustin back to Walmart, he gave Dustin twenty-four thousand and told him that I would be at the Gaylord hotel on a certain date in August. There was where he should do the job. This reference to my stay at the Gaylord reminds me of something that had previously slipped my mind. I remember that after I checked out, I spent time comforting an upset friend. We talked in her room until quite late. Finally, around 1:30 a.m., we called for a bellman to walk us to our cars in the parking garage. My friend was so concerned for our safety that she looked under the cars and in the back seats for any ne'er-do-wells who might be waiting to pounce us. In retrospect, I wonder if one of John's felon cohorts was there. Maybe they got tired of waiting for me.

Dustin Hiroms

But instead of going to the Gaylord, Dustin says he went back to East Texas, where he met two new friends, Jason Rendine and Stephanie Delacerda, and got high. Dustin gave Jason a thousand "just because." He also went to meet his grandmother, Barbara Hiroms, at a church, intending to give her ten-thousand dollars. Unfortunately, Dustin says he put the money "on the roof" (I assume he means the roof of the car.) while he went to talk to Barbara. Then they drove off without retrieving the money.

The more Dustin says, the more outlandish the story becomes. Who in his right mind would leave that much money sitting on the hood of a car and then forget about it? But obviously, Dustin wasn't in his right mind. Maybe all that dope fried his brain.

The next part of Dustin's story is more ridiculous than the last. He describes his last trip to Carrollton, to pick up money from John at our house. Along with his new friend Jason, Dustin drove around our neighborhood looking for our house. He was supposed to pick up five hundred dollars at the meter box in the alley, behind the house. Dustin explains that Billie told him he had used that location to pick up money from John. Apparently in desperation, Dustin and Jason got out of the car and began running between houses—looking for the right one. (I must admit, this testimony leads to a bit of comic relief as I picture this tall lanky kid who appears to be no more than twelve years old but thinks of himself as a hitman!)

Their quest was interrupted by the police, who picked them up for suspicious activity. Dustin's first explanation for his actions was that he was coming to see his cousin, but he can't remember his other explanations. Finally, he told the police that he was a "hit man" but didn't tell them anything else. Unfortunately, he was so high that he wasn't believable. He was then arrested and surrendered the meth he was carrying and his cell phone.

After further testimony about Dustin's meetings with John, more cash payments, and a couple of wired payments to the bank account of Dustin's grandmother, the prosecutor adds up the total that John paid Dustin: forty thousand in cash and seven thousand in wired payments.

Dustin's testimony is interrupted by a prolonged discussion, sometimes more of a debate, among the attorneys and the judge regarding cell phone numbers, screenshots of phones, and texts. While they're wrangling, I almost doze off until I hear one attorney mention "Jose." I gather from what they say that Dustin's name for John in his phone was "Jose." For the second time today, I smile.

The prosecutor introduces another exhibit, number 130, a note from Dustin to his neighbor. The note has the name "Jose" along with one of John's phone numbers, numbers of bail bondsmen, and a number for Dustin's attorney. The neighbor is instructed to call Jose for money if Dustin is ever in jail.

After Dustin's testimony that he never used drugs with or sold drugs to John, Dustin answers the defense attorney's questions about his own drug use, which was daily. The next questions make clear that Frank's attorney is attacking Dustin's credibility because the answers reveal that Dustin is currently in jail. After the court allows Dustin to consult with his attorney, Dustin explains that he is charged with aggravated assault with a deadly weapon—assault against his grandmother, Barbara Hiroms. Because Barbara has been a witness for the state, the defense attorney argues that he should be allowed to ask if the assault had anything to do with the current case.

Dustin's explanation is rather comical to me. Apparently, he was arguing with his brother Joe about repairing Barbara's television. When she came home, she got mad at Dustin for being on the roof. Dustin and Joe started fighting, and when she "stepped in," Dustin knocked a hole in the wall. The kids next door called the police. When they arrived, Dustin was outside smoking a cigarette and refused to throw it down. They then cuffed him, and in his pocket, they found a knife—the "deadly weapon."

The prosecutor introduces State's Exhibit 73, which contains screen shots of Dustin's text messages to John. Addressing the recipient as "Jose," one message reads, "Couldn't find her Saturday.... Still in Terrell.... So let me know some info of the ins and outs. Thanks, bubba, I got your back." When asked what he meant by "ins" and "outs," Dustin says he wanted to know my schedule. In another message to Jose, Dustin writes, "I need at least forty thousand to get out.... I need to know what time she leaves tomorrow so I can make my move."

Listening to one message after another, I wish I had a remote control that could mute the microphone at the witness stand. Thankfully, "Jose's" responses to the messages were deleted because, as Dustin explains, his phone was set to automatically delete incoming messages. Like the defense attorney, I wonder why he didn't delete his outgoing messages, which are certainly incriminating. I would love to delete the last three days of this torture.

I am surprised to hear a new name mentioned that I don't remember hearing—Loy Petty. According to Dustin, Petty knew about the murder-for-hire plan and was going with Dustin to tell me about the plan. (I'm losing count of how many other people knew.) When the defense attorney asks when they were going to tell me, Dustin says within a couple of weeks, that is, when he had gotten all the money from John that he could get. Dustin justifies the delay, saying, "If I was getting all the money, then she wouldn't be in danger... because he was only focused on me." Of course, in retrospect, I probably wouldn't have believed the story even if I had been told. Had Dustin confessed to me that Frank (or John) wanted me dead, I would have considered him insane.

However, Dustin declares that he knew what kind of car I drove, a blue Buick. Okay, he's becoming more believable. He explains that he saw pictures of my car when he was at Michael Speck's house. Hearing all these revelations, I feel violated—over and over—and reach for a lemon drop.

CHAPTER 21

Charlie, a Maverick Felon

Another bail bondsman, Jim Morgan, briefly testifies to having received a wire transfer from Snew Management Company for twenty-five thousand to post bond for Billie Earl. Billie's daughter, Jessica Johnson, is called next and corroborates what other witnesses have said about getting money from John and receiving wired money into her bank account. I begin to feel numb to the tedious repetition of the state's evidence. Will I always be pained by what is becoming increasingly clear: Frank was doling out thousands of dollars to have me killed?

Jessica describes the same vagabond lifestyle that seems normal for many previous witnesses, especially Billie Earl's clan and hangers on. She has gone from living with her grandparents, to living with Jennifer Northcutt (her friend), next with Billie and Stacey, and then with a fellow named Charlie Louderman. Like many other witnesses, she confesses to using drugs, which her dad supplied, as well as to being arrested. (I cannot imagine a father more reprehensible than Billie. And for Frank even to know a person like Billie is unthinkable.)

Jessica's testimony is followed by that of Charles Louderman. Charlie is a stocky man with a focused expression, suggesting to me that he may be more intelligent than most of the other clowns in this black comedy. Charlie's description of his first meeting with Billie Earl is quite colorful. Billie came up to Charlie's house "at the top of a dead end road," riding a loud motorcycle,

> a deep, deep purple, Dave Bourget outlaw chopper.... [Billie] had on black chaps over his pants, black boots. He had on a black vest over a Stroker's T-shirt, no helmet, and sunglasses with a bandana tied around his neck.

Charlie goes on to describe his first conversation with Billie, who told him that he had learned from some people in the area that Charlie could acquire firearms for him. When asked if he and Billie had become friends, Charlie answers, "acquaintances with reservations." (Again, I get a bit of a chuckle as his deep voice and serious expression reveal no hint of sarcasm.) Billie started paying him seven hundred dollars a week to "watch over his daughter and be his runner and gopher." Asked to explain what he was running, Charlie gives this account:

> If his bike broke down, I would...go get his bike no matter where it was. If he needed firearms, if he needed assistance anywhere. If somebody was threatening him, his wife...I mean his ex-wife, her family, his two sons, if his dog needed fed....watched a lot of Billie's boats, his four-wheelers, enclosed trailers, motorcycle trailers, the motorcycle sometimes, yeah.

Charlie was in his front yard with Billie the first time that he heard John Howard. Because Charlie had repeatedly asked Billie where he was getting all his money, Billie put John on speakerphone. Billie told John that Charlie was listening and introduced Charlie as "Bud." Billie then asked John to reassure Charlie that Billie was not an undercover law enforcement officer or a drug dealer. On the other end of the phone, John started laughing and said Billie was no kind of cop.

After explaining times when he contacted John to bail Billie out of jail, Charlie describes an occasion when he accompanied Billie to pick up a picture from John. John, who was driving a Lexus, gave Billie an envelope with five thousand and a cell phone with a large screen. On the phone was a picture of John "with a very happy, cheerful-looking lady...who looked like she should be his wife." Billie told Charlie that the picture was to "I.D. the mark"—that is, "the target."

Charlie then tells of another time when he was with Billie, who put John on speakerphone. Charlie heard John say "he was going to a Mavericks game, that his wife would be home alone, and that if he wouldn't be back until a certain time that evening, ...would that be enough time."

Hearing this, I remember another time I was alone. At a craft retreat, I was the last person to leave. When I got to my car and tried to start it, I discovered the battery was dead. Because it was relatively new, I was surprised. Looking back, I wonder if someone had tampered with the battery. All the knowledge that these conspirators had about my locations horrifies me, as I consider how many close calls I may have had.

My attention turns back to Charlie, who continues his account of John's instructions: If Billie didn't have enough time to kill me when John was at a game, he could find me eating with friends on, "I forget if it was a Tuesday or Thursday night, at a restaurant in town with a table right at one of the front windows."

Charlie mentions other schedules that John was concerned about, such as when our daughter would come in from college, or when he would be in Kuwait, or when the neighbors were having company. When Charlie is then asked if John ever said how the hit should be done, he says it should look like an accident. The next details that Charlie provides are chilling:

> *Like the restaurant with the window, it was to be a fully automatic weapon, and that way you pull up and look at the target....The first fire goes to the target, and then you spray around. And that way your target is eliminated and it looks like an innocent person in a drive-by shooting.*

Charlie also tells of John' suggestion of how Billie could make the hit look like a robbery:

> *When he told us he would be gone and the alarm would be off, he give[me] the code for the entry to the garage... and that in the middle of his wife's—I think it was her dresser in her bedroom, there would be a jewelry box with at least $40,000 worth of gold and silver.*

My throat closes up. My eye tears. This information had to have come from Frank although he exaggerated the value of my jewelry. Once again, my chest tightens as I face the growing mound of evidence against Frank. The truth is searing. I have been living with a cold-hearted man set on killing me—at any cost. A lemon drop falls to the floor.

The prosecutor seems to strengthen his case when he submits State's Exhibit 162, a picture of John Howard in the black Lexus with Billie on the Dave Bourget outlaw chopper, which he had earlier ridden to Charlie's place. (I wonder if the defense attorney will ask the circumstances in which the picture was taken.) But for now, the prosecutor asks if on speakerphone or in person Charlie ever heard John express frustration with Billie. He answers by relaying John's angry question of why Billie was taking so long, why he couldn't get it done. As Charley explains, John's irritation was evident as he fumed over all the money he'd spent: "I've spent a lot of money. You know you told me you were going to do it this time....I've bailed you out of jail. I've helped you....This is financially draining me."

After confirming that Billie once brought a bag of money for him to protect, Charlie is asked whether John ever talked about getting a divorce or having a girlfriend. About having a girlfriend, John admitted he did and that that he was spending a lot of money on having two relationships. (I guess Frank thought he needed to get rid of one—me.) According to Charlie, John told Billie he was not considering a divorce because the insurance on me would double in the case of accidental death.

Charlie asserts that although Billie didn't do the hit, he acted like he would:

> He would order different weapons depending on if she was supposed to be at her house or at a restaurant.... He would buy Ronsonal fuel, things like that, duct tape, gloves, jogging suits, masks, Tasers, everything...tools of the trade to get the job done.

The defense attorney later asks why Billie bought Rononal fuel. The answer—"To burn the house down and everything in it."

Charlie's testimony takes an interesting turn when he recounts Billie's first story about the target for the hit: a member of the Aryan Brotherhood who had raped an oilfield man's daughter. When Charlie found out that I was the real target, he didn't want to be involved. He says that after he saw a picture of me, he told John on the phone that "he was a chickensh—t." Although killing a rapist was okay with him, Charlie says, "If I had to pay that much money to kill my wife, I'd do it myself."

At that point, Charlie says he and Billie parted ways, a matter of concern to John because he feared that Charlie couldn't be trusted. In fact, Charlie asserts that he told an investigator in the Wood County Sheriff's Department about Billie's plan. As a result, Billie and Stacey Serenko were investigated and kept in the sheriff's custody for more than two days (another chance to stop the plan that goes nowhere). The prosecutor ends his questioning through a series of questions and answers explaining how Michael Speck (Billie's nephew) obtained a 22-automatic Browning.

The defense attorney begins his cross examination of Charlie by asking his first impression of Billie. Charlie says he thought Billie was a member of some Texas syndicate because he had longhorns on his motorcycle. (I continue to be astounded by this underworld of criminals that I had never heard of. I guess I lived a very protected life before August 18, 2012.)

The usual questions about dope follow, the culmination of which confirms Billie's possession of large quantities of drugs. Charlie also reveals that Billie got his daughter, Jessica, hooked on drugs and kept her high (more evidence that Billie should never have spawned a child). Another revelation is that Charlie had told a Detective Turner about Billie's involvement with drugs and the murder conspiracy.

Charlie also told the detective his low opinion of Billie's son Derrick, his belief that anybody in the Johnson clan would sell "somebody down the river in a heartbeat," and his opinion that Stacey Serenko was as involved as Billie in the conspiracy. Furthermore, Charlie acknowledges describing Stacey as "sweet as anybody," but she could "turn on you like a rattlesnake." He even says that he believed Stacey was going to kill Billie. As for the murder-for-hire deal, Charlie acknowledges that he was prepared to be involved only when he thought the target was the person who raped John's daughter.

Before the defense attorney finishes the cross examination, court is adjourned, but the next day of the trial Charlie is again called to the stand. The defense resumes questioning Charlie. He asks why John continued talking with Charlie after Charlie insulted him. "Because Billie told me to shut up," Charlie answers. Charlie also admits to being on probation for ten years, for firing a weapon in public.

Another admission from Charlie—his anger at Billie for threatening his (Charlie's) family. He told Billie if he ever spoke to him again he would dig up Billie's brother who had just died and chain him to his truck and drag him through the middle of town. (I wonder if the jury is thinking what I'm thinking. Is the guy for real?)

When the defense attorney asks Charlie if he ever told anyone about a Hummer in our garage, Charlie says he can't remember. His excuse is an "altercation with a man ten months ago," when he was hit in the head with some brass knuckles. Charlie claims that sometimes his eye starts twitching, which can affect his memory. (A blow to the head leading to a twitching eye that causes memory loss—I'm impressed by Charlie's imaginative diagnosis of his cognitive problems.)

After the defense attorney finishes, the prosecutor asks how John reacted when he called him a chickensh—t." Charlie replies that John got real quiet and then said, "Billie, Billie, Billie." And Billie said, "Charlie, we don't talk to our clients like that," to which Charlie replied, "He ain't my client."

The final questions elicit confirmation that Billie never supplied John with drugs, that Charlie never saw John do drugs, and that he never heard Billie and John discussing going in to business together.

I watch as Charlie exits the witness stand and passes by the row where I am seated. I'm surprised when he makes eye contact and gives me a nod. Hummm.....It makes me think he's glad he backed out when he saw my picture.

CHAPTER 22

A Blackmail Scheme

D ouglas Mulder, a Dallas attorney, is the next witness for the state. Mulder was a prosecutor under Henry Wade, a former Dallas district attorney. Mulder reports that Billie hired him to represent him in a Dallas County case and told him to contact his CPA for payment. When Mulder called the number Billie gave him, a man named John (no last name was given) asked for wiring instructions to Mulder's bank. A few days later, Mulder's account received payment for representing Billie. The cover sheet for the transfer indicated that the payment came from Snew Management Company, an organization that Mulder had never heard of. Another puzzle piece in the picture connecting Frank/John to the phone numbers and money.

A Carrollton police officer, Amber Maher, is called to testify about a traffic stop she and another officer made less than two weeks before the shooting. At 1:00 a.m., she and Officer Burham saw a car that they had noticed earlier. When they spotted the expired registration, they decided to pull the car over to investigate. The officers questioned the two occupants separately, Dustin Hiroms and Anthony Jason Rendine. Because they gave conflicting stories about why they were in that neighborhood (very close to my house), the officers arrested the pair on unrelated charges.

Before I have time to wonder why Officer Maher's testimony is so brief, the prosecutor calls Stephanie Delacerda Rendine to the stand. Stephanie appears to be very nervous, for the prosecutor kindly tells her to take a deep breath. Stephanie, the wife of Jason Rendine, has three grown daughters and is employed at North Park Mall. Asked when and how she met Dustin Hiroms, she says the meeting occurred on July 4, 2012.

Stephanie, Jason, and Jason's daughter, Caitlyn, had built a bonfire for roasting weenies and marshmallows. When Dustin drove by their house, he stopped because he saw a neighbor he knew. Dustin got out of his car and introduced himself. Then Dustin reached in his pocket and gave Stephanie five or six 100-dollar bills and said, "Happy Fourth of July." He also gave Caitlyn two 100-dollar bills and a thousand dollars each to Jason and the neighbor.

Later when Stephanie walked in the house, she saw Dustin and the neighbor counting money—thousands of dollars laid out on her bed—while Jason was playing a computer game. That same night she and Jason smoked methamphetamine with Dustin. Stephanie also acknowledges that she stayed under the influence of the drug for several days. She says that around July 12 or 13 that Jason left with Dustin to go to Dallas, presumably to "score on some methamphetamine." After getting out of jail a few days later, Jason returned, with John's phone number and the knowledge of the murder-for-hire plan. (So, here's another person privy to the plan. How could so many people know without someone intervening?)

With that information, Jason and Stephanie hatched a plan to blackmail John. Using the fictitious names of Wes and Tiffany, they called John and threatened to tell the police about the murder plan. According to Stephanie, John asked "Tiffany" what it would take for her not to contact the police. When Stephanie, acting as Tiffany, didn't give an amount, John said to meet him at a Whataburger in Garland, in front of a Fry's store. When John arrived in a "grayish, bluish kind of metallic-looking Lexus," Jason walked over to the car and was handed a white envelope containing three thousand dollars. John told them he would call in a few days and give them more money.

A day or two later, Stephanie met John at the same place and received an envelope with twelve thousand. Shortly thereafter, Jason and Stephanie ran out of money and called John again. This time John said he was in California, so he would wire money to Stephanie (alias Tiffany). Because she had no bank account, Stephanie had to set one up, at Wells Fargo. The prosecutor then introduces a copy of the wire transaction, for twenty thousand from Genshcu Management Company.

Because Stephanie had to use her real name to open a bank account, she concocted a story to explain why the wire didn't go to Tiffany. She told John that Stephanie was her sister and that Tiffany and Wes were on the run from the law and that they owed a drug dealer six thousand dollars. Stephanie further claimed that she knew what was going on (the murder plan) and that Tiffany had told her that John would take care of everything. Stephanie also told John that she worked for a defense attorney in Dallas. To that, John asked her if she knew anyone who "could take care of it" (the murder), a question he had also asked "Wes" and "Tiffany." John seemed frustrated when he kept getting "no" for an answer.

For the next meeting with John, Stephanie went as herself, by disguising herself with different hair color, more upscale clothing, and a more upscale car than when she went as Tiffany. John was fooled into giving Stephanie ten thousand to take care of Wes and Tiffany's debt and to help Stephanie buy an RV. Stephanie met John one more time to get another ten thousand, supposedly to help her move to Louisiana.

I'm mentally trying to add up all this money that Stephanie and Jason extorted from Frank. I'm still amazed at these characters' cunning and Frank's gullibility. As I sneak a quick look at Frank, I see no sign of any embarrassment or discomfort; instead he sits erect with folded hands and unbowed head.

Stephanie's testimony takes an interesting turn when she's asked if she and Jason had ever seen my house. Not only did she see the house but also took a picture of it and knocked on the door. She even used the Internet to find the number of our landline. She called that number several times but got only voice mail and hung up without leaving a message. She explains her reason for trying to contact me: "My conscience was bothering me, and I wanted to let her know what was going on." Stephanie also claims that she told police about the murder plot, but they didn't believe her.

The prosecutor next introduces exhibits showing text messages between Stephanie and John, mostly describing when and where to meet. The questioning turns to Stephanie and Jason's arrest in Louisiana four days after the shooting. They were picked up on a BOLO (be-on-the-lookout) for their car, the same one that had been stopped by the two officers in my neighborhood before the shooting. Stephanie and Jason were charged with possession of marijuana and methamphetamine. At that time, Stephanie says she didn't even know about the shooting. When questioned by the police about her involvement with John Howard, she lied by saying she was having an affair with him.

When Stephanie was later questioned by Carrollton police, she asserts that she told the truth because it was only then that she learned about the shooting and only then that she had an attorney. And it was then that she was off drugs. She also says, "No," to a range of questions: Did she ever do drugs with or provide drugs to John? Did John ever suggest going into a legitimate business? Did she know Billie Earl or his children, Stacey Serenko, or Robert Merrill? Did John ever threaten to tell the police about her blackmailing him?

In the cross examination, the defense attorney begins listing Stephanie's lies, one that the prosecutor had not mentioned. When first questioned in Louisiana about the money she had, she said that it was from a business transaction. He also reveals her convictions of forgery in 1992 and robbery in 1994 and 1997, after which she served ten years in prison. Furthermore, he contends that she told the Louisiana police that she got the money for oral sex, not from an affair. These accusations Stephanie does not dispute, nor does she dispute that she is guilty of blackmail. She does emphatically dispute that she was involved in any way with the shooting.

Stephanie then describes her numerous attempts to contact me about the threat to my life: using a track search to find different businesses that John was in, calling and going to many such businesses in the hope that I might be working for John, waiting outside my house in the hope that I would come home. She even says that a search of her computer will prove her attempts to find me.

The defense attorney then questions Stephanie about her motive for testifying, suggesting that she was getting a deal or hoped to get a deal in return for her testimony. She denies that she knows anything about such a deal and gives this as her motive:

> For two years, I have lived with this, and I've been a nervous wreck ever since. And I have this hanging over my head, and I've lost everything I ever had before John Howard and everything since then, including my moral that I ever had.

When the defense attorney questions her morals, she asserts that after coming out of the penitentiary, she worked hard to build a new reputation. She worked years for the same company, she raised her children and they knew where she was every night, and she wasn't on drugs. The attorney ends his cross examination by repeating the different lies she had told as well as her frequent memory lapses. Stephanie again emphasizes that she had told police about the murder plan even before the shooting. (I still can't understand why no one connected the dots until it was too late.)

After Stephanie is excused, her husband, Jason Rendine, is sworn in as a witness for the state. The initial series of questions and answers confirm Stephanie's description of their first meetings with Dustin Hiroms and the trip to Dallas that Jason took with Dustin. Jason also says that on the trip he heard Dustin's conversation with John on speakerphone about picking up money at the meter box behind John's house. When Jason asked Dustin what was going on, Dustin told him that John was paying his family to kill his wife.

During that unfruitful search for John's house, Dustin stopped at a 7-Eleven. When Dustin went inside, Jason looked at Dustin's phone and copied down the number of the last call. Later after the Carrollton police pulled them over, Jason was arrested for an unpaid traffic violation in Dallas. He was soon released because the Dallas police refused to come after him.

Jason describes walking to the DART station in Carrollton and taking two different train lines to Garland, where his uncle and aunt picked him up. Jason says he told them both about the murder plan. And when his employer and his wife, Ernie and Jane, took Jason back to East Texas, Jason told them as well. He also gave them John's number and asked them to call the police, which a police sergeant later confirms. When he got home, he and Stephanie quickly devised the blackmail scheme, hoping to get money from John before the police got to him. (Okay, now I'm beginning to wonder if there were any people in Billie's widening sphere of influence who were ignorant of the murder plan.)

The rest of the blackmail story that Jason tells corroborates Stephanie's account. Jason also confirms the proposition from John that Stephanie had explained: John would pay Jason fifty thousand to find someone to kill me and a hundred thousand to the person who did it. Although Jason declares that he never planned to take the deal, he continued to tell John he was working on it. Jason describes John as "persistent" in that request.

Asked about the last time he saw Dustin, Jason says that Dustin came to the house after they had been arrested and released in Carrollton. When he arrived, Jason told Dustin not to come around again. Jason also denies knowing any of Billie's or Stacey Serenko's families.

A series of text messages between John and Jason is the focus of the next questions. The defense attorney asks why several of those messages deal with what my schedule was at various times. Why would Jason and John be communicating on that subject if Jason wasn't serious about helping John get me killed? Jason continues to insist that he was merely placating John, to get more money. To further questions about lies that Jason told authorities, he maintains that he was afraid and that he worried about not having a lawyer. Jason admits, however, that he has been charged with solicitation to commit murder and is currently out on bond with a leg monitor. He also denies that he has a deal in return for his testimony.

CHAPTER 23

The Hit

S till another witness for the state is called, Loy Petty. A next-door neighbor of Barbara Hiroms, Petty describes his going with Dustin Hiroms to get money from his "Uncle" John. Petty says they drove to Town East Mall where they met a man at Sheplers. Although Petty did not see the man, he was in a Lexus and gave Dustin ten thousand dollars in hundreds.

When asked by the defense attorney if he did drugs, Loy says, "No," but acknowledges that Dustin did. To the attorney's question about Dustin's reputation, especially whether he was known to lie a lot, Loy answers that he knows only that Dustin is an idiot. He gives as an example Dustin's telling people he's a hit man. As Loy suggests, only an idiot would do that. (My earlier impression of Dustin is confirmed.)

A crucial witness for the prosecution is next: Misti Ford, who had been engaged to a man named Michael Lorence. Misti testifies that Lorence became friends with Billie's nephew, Michael Speck, when they were in prison together. In June of 2012, two months before the shooting, Lorence was released from prison and went to live with Misti. On August 14, 2012, Speck sent them money to come to visit him in Grand Saline, Texas, "to catch up." (Lorence was planning to ask Speck to be his best man.) A day later, they drove for twenty-four hours from Misti's home in California to Grand Saline.

When they arrived in Texas on August 16, they rented a Nissan Altima from Hertz and returned it on August 20, 2012. The prosecutor provides the rental information in State's Exhibit 47, which also gives the license number of the car. When asked why they rented a car, Misti says that Lorence thought it was a good idea not to put the miles on her car, especially since she had a bad tire.

After they arrived in Grand Saline, they stayed with Speck, his wife, and his son. A couple of days later, Lorence and Speck left in the rental car for Dallas, where they said they would do some sightseeing and "side jobs." They left on August 18 before Misti woke up. When they returned around

11:00 that night, Lorence and Speck started drinking, and Lorence was uncharacteristically quiet. Misti says, normally "he doesn't ever shut up."

Asked if Lorence told her anything that would "subject him to criminal prosecution," Misti is finally allowed to answer after the defense attorney's objections are overruled: "He said that he had murdered somebody..., a female." He said he "shot her in her garage in the forehead." Upon hearing this, Misti says she started crying and went for a walk.

The prosecutor then shows Misti pictures of the church parking lot and the Altima, which she identifies as the one she and Lorence had rented. When asked why she didn't immediately tell the police, Misti says she was afraid of Lorence. To the prosecutor's question, "What were you afraid of," she answers, "of the same thing happening to me." (For a moment, I feel a kinship with Misti. Her fear is familiar to me, painfully familiar.)

Cross examination of Misti is brief. She reveals that Speck sent them money to come to Texas so that they would bring Speck's brother with them. She testifies further that they received no money from Speck after they returned to California. She also reveals that she left Lorence on October 8, two months after the shooting and never told anyone about it until authorities questioned her in January, 2013, months after the shooting.

Here comes another witness for the state. How many more can the jury endure? I know I'm worn out from the interminable string of witnesses. I'm also having trouble keeping up with who is related to whom. I hope this witness is not a relative of Billie Earl.

Thankfully the witness being sworn in is a law enforcement officer with the city of Carrollton, Matt Burnham He is the one who, with Officer Amber Maher, picked up Jason Rendine and Dustin Hiroms when they were trying to find my house. Burnham says that after Dustin's conflicting stories about what they were doing in that neighborhood, Dustin said he was a hit man, that he needed to meet a man named John and pick up some money, and that the house he was looking for was "off Bluebonnet." Dustin also explains that the money he needed to pick up was in an electrical box.

When asked what he did with the information from Dustin, Officer Burnham gives this account:

> *I kind of didn't believe him.... He admitted to smoking meth. He was kind of coming down off his high. The stories that he had told us leading*

up to [saying he was a hit man] were kind of crazy. So, I just basically put it in the back of my mind, really didn't do anything that night.

I know we requested another officer to check electrical boxes in the area, but he didn't find anything. So, there was really nothing at that point to kind of validate the story he was giving. It wasn't until a little bit later that I started becoming concerned with the story.

Another officer is then sworn in. Cory Gardner, an officer in the Carrollton Police Department, is an intel detective, which he describes as a jack-of-all-trades. He was tasked with laying out a visual representation of data from phone records. Gardner set up a correlation between Michael Speck's phone number and two other phone records over a ten-day span—to determine the time and duration of calls and texts. The main point of all this testimony seems to be documenting the phone communication between Michael Speck and Frank on the day of the shooting.

Jeffrey Shaffer is recalled as a witness. A member of the Secret Service, he is the digital forensic lab manager for North Texas Electronic Crimes Task Force. After some testimony explaining how time discrepancies in phones can occur, Shaffer is asked to read an incoming text on May 7, 2012, from a South Tahoe cell (presumably Suzanne's text to John's cell):

I'm so sick of being alone. You need to file [for divorce] by this Friday or move on. I have waited long enough. Heard all the same bulls—t for three years.... You are just protecting yourself because you can't face your family. Because of all the time that has passed, your family will never accept me and you f—king know it. You have talked about our future only getting my hopes up.... It is my fault because I wanted to believe you. I'm so sick of worrying about you having a heart attack or stroke because you are so stressed.... It is now or never, your choice.

Shaffer reads another text sent on May 30, 2012, from the same South Tahoe number to John's cell:

You have a real issue with me asking you about filing your papers. I really want an answer. You get so defensive that I know you're hiding something. You have no right getting mad at me or giving me your attitude. Now is the time for you to grow up and deal with your sh—t one way or another.

Then on August 12, comes another text from Suzanne, "We need to talk," and on August 13, 2012, "What did I do wrong? I'm so upset.... I love you."

Wow! Suzanne was really putting the pressure on Frank. Typical Frank— avoid confrontation. Gosh! Despite living two lives, Frank is remarkably consistent. Although I would never give Frank an ultimatum like Suzanne seemed to do, she and I have this similarity: She's in California and not getting what she wants, and I'm in Texas not getting what I want. I wonder what Frank is thinking now. Again, I glance his way but see only that stoic posture and the folded hands.

CHAPTER 24

Ramping up the Investigation

The next witness I have come to know well. Detective Michael Wall of the Carrollton Police Department has been the lead investigator in the case. He has had the uncomfortable task of explaining to me all the evidence against Frank. He begins his testimony by describing his initial investigation: securing the crime scene, determining Frank's whereabouts, obtaining a search warrant of our house, and locating my purse in a dumpster close by. In examining the purse and finding the contents intact, Wall and other investigators realized that robbery was not the motive.

The next day after finding the taco bag I had thrust at the shooter, Wall discovered the time-stamped receipt, which enabled him to pinpoint the time of the attack. He also reviewed the church video that showed a vehicle following my car. When Frank returned from California, Wall asked him to come to the police station for an interview.

During the interview the next day, Frank agreed to an analysis of his cell phone and to provide his DNA. He also complied with the request to bring in his laptop computer. Wall testifies that Frank said he had been working with Richard Raley in California when the shooting occurred. When asked if he knew Billie Earl Johnson, Stacey Serenko, Michael Speck, or any other involved characters, Frank said, "No."

The prosecutor submits State's Exhibit 64, a disk containing copies of two phone calls from the Denton County jail, one from Stacey on June 4, and one from Billie on July 31—both in 2012. And both calls were made to John Howard. In Stacey's call, she tells John that Michael Speck "is ready to go" if one of them (she or Billie) could get out of jail. She says, "We can make it happen tomorrow." To that, John asks for Michael's phone number. Detective Wall repeats that in the interview Frank never mentioned those calls. After the analysis of Frank's phone, Wall says he contacted the FBI and asked them to question Suzanne Leontieff, who turned over her cell phones and letters from Frank Howard.

Wall then followed up on a tip from Detective Burnham, who thought the earlier traffic stop of Jason Rendine and Dustin Hiroms might be relevant. Armed with that information, Wall was able to locate Rendine and

Stephanie Delacerda in Bossier Parish, Louisiana, where they had been arrested on unrelated charges. Wall says that when he went there to interview them, he learned from Stephanie about her receiving a wire transfer of twenty thousand dollars from a company called Genschu.

The next step was discovering that John Howard was the president and registered agent for Genschu. That discovery was the first direct connection with John Franklin Howard and money paid to anyone. With that lead, the financial aspect of the investigation took off.

As Wall continues his testimony, I am dumfounded by the magnitude of the investigation, the number of interviews with so many players in this drama—the questioning of one witness after another, to verify each fact over and over. Had I been merely a bystander and not a victim in this tragedy, I would be enthralled by the doggedness of the investigators.

More information was forthcoming six days after the shooting, first from an interview with Billie Earl in the Denton County jail, an interview that Billie requested. That same day Wall says he received a report from FBI Agent DiLisi containing the information Stacey Serenko had given him. At that point, Wall says he tried unsuccessfully to contact John Franklin Howard for a follow-up interview. Wall also reveals that out of concern for my safety, he needed to inform me of the evidence against Frank. As a result, the hospital became off-limits for Frank.

On that same day, Dustin Hiroms was arrested in Tyler, and his cell phones and a scribbled note were confiscated. After an interview with Dustin, detectives were sent to the Gaylord Texas Hotel, where they obtained a receipt showing my stay there, as Dustin had maintained. That same day, August 26, 2012, Wall says he got a probable cause arrest warrant for John Franklin Howard. When police arrested Frank at our home, they also had another search warrant, which led to their confiscation of a second laptop computer. In addition, police executed search warrants for Frank's offices, where officers discovered financial records of four accounts: Genschu, Snew, Sutaho, and JFH—all tying in to the different wire transfers that police had found.

Police also found in one of the offices a wire-by-fax document addressed to Derrick Johnson. A ledger with phone numbers related to the case was another piece of evidence obtained there. This collection of evidence enabled them to get probable cause arrest warrants for Derrick Johnson and Michael Speck, Billlie's son and nephew.

The prosecutor's questions then lead to Wall's listing financial records that the grand jury subpoenaed—bank accounts of nine individuals, including Frank Howard's, Richard Raley's, and many who were involved with wire transfers from Howard's managed accounts. Those financial records were submitted to FBI analysts Bruce Card and Bill Brown.

Wall also lists numerous interviews conducted by various law enforcement agencies, primarily the Carrollton Police Department. According to Wall, information from those interviews was both consistent and helpful, for it led to probable cause arrest warrants for Billie Earl, Jason Rendine, and Stephanie Delacerda.

At this point, however, Wall says that the investigation stalled. I remember when Wall told me they had been unable to find the shooter, I told him I would rally my prayer group to ask for the Lord's help. Two weeks later, Wall received a phone call from a woman in California, Sherry Dominick, who provided a lead—the name of Misti Ford, Dominick's daughter. Dominick told him that Misti had confided to her sister that she was concerned about her fiancé, Michael Lorence. Because Lorence had confessed to her that he had killed a lady in Dallas, Misti was afraid of him...afraid he might kill her too.

Wall explains that this tip about Michael Lorence, a player new to the investigators, was the break they needed. After talking with Dominick, Wall could connect Michael Lorence to Michael Speck, through jail documents that showed them as cellmates. Coincidentally, Wall had just received the report on the vehicle that followed me from the church. Careful analysis of the church video finally provided a clear rendering of the license plate.

Detective Wall's testimony continues for several hours, detailing connections between phone numbers; dates, times, and recordings of phone calls; interviews and follow-up interviews; locations of cell towers; Western Union and hotel receipts; photographs; video; text messages—the list goes on and on, culminating in a power point presentation of all the data that Wall explains to the jury. One of the photographs is of me shortly after the shooting; even though I've seen it before, it still torments me.

I am overwhelmed by all this evidence presented in the power point. But to me, the most incriminating facts are the numerous calls between Michael Speck's phone and Frank's phone from August 15, 2012 to August 18, especially the call made three minutes after I phoned 911.

Michael Speck

In cross examination, the defense attorney reveals that Wall had several receipts from hotels notarized in the police department. The attorney points out that the notary was not present when the receipts were obtained and therefore are not valid. He also questions the truthfulness of the characters involved in the conspiracy. Wall's response is that corroboration among various statements and physical evidence was his method of establishing truthfulness.

My mother is the state's next witness. She testifies that in 2011, I stayed with her at her home in San Marcos after her hospitalization. Her testimony also establishes that she never knew Frank to go by any other name, that Frank had been to her house many times, and that she never knew him to be a millionaire. She also answers questions regarding my five surgeries and the physical and emotional pain I endured. Thankfully, the defense attorney chooses not to ask her any questions.

After Mother is excused, I am again called to the stand. The prosecutor asks me questions that verify testimony of other witnesses. I confirm that my tire was slashed in the summer of 2010 and that I kept my most expensive jewelry in my dresser in the master bedroom. I also confirm staying at the Gaylord Texas Hotel and Frank's asking me for my room number. Of course, I gave it to him, later thinking that maybe Frank was taking to heart what we learned from the marriage counselor: that because Frank's travel reduced our time together, he could remind me of his love by sending me cards or even flowers. Back then, I smiled, thinking that Frank might surprise me with something special—even just a single flower in a vase—as a message of "I love you."

Suddenly another memory surfaces about the Gaylord. When I first arrived, I had three women with me. Because we were running late to the conference, I let them off at the hotel entrance and then drove into the parking garage. I stayed in my car long enough to change clothes since I had not had time to put on the T-shirt we were supposed to wear. When I think about how vulnerable I was—sitting alone in my car, half dressed— I feel a panic attack coming on. But I remind myself as I have often done, that God was protecting me.

I focus again on the prosecutor's questions, which elicit from me the color of my car, the scrapbooking retreat that I attended annually, and the fact that Frank and I never had separate bedrooms. I also testify that when Frank was going through treatment for his cancer, he never showed any signs of drug addiction. (I'm surprised someone didn't think to ask for his medical records, since his blood work would very likely have revealed drugs if he had been using them.)

The defense attorney asks me if I had an insurance policy, to which I answer that Frank told me I did. I also agree that no one associated with this trial had asked me about such a policy. Although the attorney suggests that my policy had lapsed, I don't know whether that is true, but I explain that I knew where Frank kept all our important papers. Abruptly, the attorney ends his cross examination, and I am released—and relieved.

CHAPTER 25

The Defense

Before the defense begins its case, there is a hearing in open court, outside the jury, about Frank's previous co-counsel, Arch McColl, and Frank's claim for attorney-client privilege. Although both the prosecution and the defense had made many efforts to subpoena McColl, they had all gone unserved. Frank is called to the stand only for the limited purpose of the hearing.

The defense attorney asks Frank if he had ever authorized Arch McColl to make statements to anyone regarding this case. Frank says, "No." In cross examination, Frank admits that McColl had visited him at the Denton County jail, but he denies sending a message to me or to our three children through McColl. When asked if he had ever been in a meeting with McColl, Richard Raley, and others, Frank says, "Yes." The prosecutor then asks Frank if he told our children that any confession he made was a mistake; he admits saying that but explains that he meant that it was not true, that he had not made a confession. Asked if he had ever told McColl that he should be punished, the defense attorney's objection is sustained, so Frank doesn't answer.

After this bit of business, Frank is excused, and the jury is brought in.

The defense attorney calls Stephanie Delacerda Rendine. The first questions she's asked have to do with two photos of her, one photo in which she is obviously heavier than in the other. The attorney's main point seems to be that Stephanie's weight couldn't have changed that much in the five to six weeks she was in contact with John—presumably casting doubt on her claim to have represented herself as two people during the blackmail scheme that she and Jason hatched. However, the attorney ends his questioning before making that point clear to the jury.

Then comes Billie Earl, sauntering into the courtroom, as a witness for the defense. Billie admits writing a letter to John's lawyer, Arch McColl, stating that on his property he had a lock box full of evidence against John Howard. In the letter, Billie threatens to turn that evidence over to the state if McColl doesn't get him out of jail. Both statements, Billie acknowledges, were untrue.

Billie is such a liar. If he were the only witness against Frank, or even if his whole family were the only witnesses, this trial probably wouldn't be happening.

Another example of Billie's cavalier attitude toward truth comes when the defense asks the next question: "Did you ever tell Arch McColl that if you didn't get out [of jail], you would have five to seven people testify...that he wanted his wife killed." Again, Billie admits writing that. He also admits stating that his family would do whatever he asked, "that he ran his circle."

The prosecutor then points out that Billie also stated that if he does get out, nobody will testify against John. (I am amused by Billie's response to the prosecutor's next question—"Were you basically promising Mr. McColl that you would intimidate the witnesses and prevent them from coming to court?" Billie asks for the question to be repeated, saying he didn't quite hear the first part. Only after the prosecutor rewords the question does Billy seem to understand. I think he just doesn't know what "intimidate" means because he answers that he could keep the witnesses from telling the truth.)

After a brief testimony by Stacey Serenko verifying when she first met Billie and when the plot began, answers consistent with her first testimony, the defense calls our children to the stand—the youngest being first. She testifies that she never saw Frank being violent to me. Asked whether there was any special security "for Frank's presence at [her] wedding," she says that she didn't know of any.

The prosecutor's questions and her answers all emphasize her lack of knowledge regarding Frank's "other life"—his affair, his lavish spending on his mistress, and all the players in the murder-for-hire drama. I only wish that she could have remained in the dark. Even more, I wish for no darkness.

Our older daughter is the next witness for the defense. She describes her father's "demeanor" at the hospital the day after the attack. He was crying and wouldn't eat, and he collapsed in the hall. He was so upset that she and her two siblings had to help him up to go into my room. She also confirms that she never saw Frank violent toward me and that she knew nothing about his affair until he told her. The subject of her sister's wedding prompts the last question: whether I had asked Frank to dance. She answers that I asked whether I should ask for a dance.

During cross examination, the prosecutor asks numerous questions concerning her prior knowledge of Frank's affair, of the various participants connected with the shooting, of the companies that wired money to those participants, and of several different phones and phone numbers. To all these queries, she says, "No." She also affirms that she never saw her father using drugs or alcohol, or cursing.

I cringe when her testimony reveals that she, her husband, and some friends had stayed in her dad's Lake Tahoe condo when they were on a skiing trip. I could not fathom how she could sleep in the same bed that her father and mistress had occupied. I felt betrayed—again. She also says that she blamed neither me nor her father for the divorce. Only one more question, this from the defense: "Do you believe your dad had your mother shot?"

"No, I do not." That answer continues to echo in my mind.

The last witness for the defense is our son, who confirms the testimony of his sister regarding our family history, Frank's behavior after the shooting, and his own lack of prior knowledge about the affair and the shady cast of characters connected with the crime. He also repeats his sister's assertion that after the shooting Frank seemed cooperative with the police.

The cross examination of our son is lengthy. One of the prosecutor's first points is my son's failure to notify police after his dad told him about his affair. My son testifies that Frank mentioned many times wanting to "kill the bastard" who had shot me, and wanting to offer a reward for finding the shooter. However, he says that Detective Wall told him a reward was unnecessary.

Concerning his dad's affair, our son admits being surprised because he had always known his dad to be truthful. He also reports his dad telling him

> [Son], just assume for logical purposes that I'm lying and work off that assumption instead of working off the more emotional assumption of I'm telling the truth. Because at this point that's going to be better for you, to figure out if I'm lying or not.

With that admission, the prosecutor passes the witness to the defense, who follows up by suggesting that Frank would not tell his son if he had been involved with a drug ring. He asks what prompted his dad to get a lawyer, to which he answers that he and his siblings did.

The prosecutor's next questions reinforce Frank's good reputation and straight-laced behavior. The prosecutor also refers to our son's statement to police, that his parents did not consider divorce an option. To that point, the defense counters with the rhetorical question—did our son know his dad had been previously divorced. Then the final question—"Do you believe your dad had anything to do with having your mother shot?"

"Absolutely not!"

After our son leaves the witness stand, the defense rests.

With the jury outside the courtroom, the defense calls Frank to testify only that he has been informed of his right to decide whether to testify in the case. He chooses not to testify. Hearing that, I lose my last hope, hope I didn't realize I had been secretly harboring—that Frank would get up on that witness stand and somehow convince me he had not wanted me dead. Lemon drops won't be enough this time. I reach for the junior mints.

The discussion that follows involves more double talk than Frank's testifying that he won't testify. The defense asks for an instructed verdict of not guilty. I believe their argument relates to their interpretation of the way the charge against Frank is worded. The defense seems to believe that "renumerated" in the charge relates to Frank's being renumerated. The state argues that it relates to someone else being renumerated. All the arguments beyond that one are way over my head.

After what seems to be hours of more bickering, the court overrules the defense's objections, although by this time I have lost track of what those objections are. Finally, I hear my favorite words: "We'll be in recess until tomorrow morning."

That night, August 18, 2014, at 10:27 (exactly two years after my world exploded), I write in my prayer journal. I have been praying in my mind for over an hour:

> *Father, I'm so thankful you walk with me. Lord God, I'm just physically sick as I think about tomorrow and closing arguments. I feel like I'm going to a funeral. Today was excruciating as my children got up one by one and testified for their father, yet I cannot be angry.... He was a good father...**was** being the operative word. God, I ask forgiveness if I'm wrong, but I truly believe Frank did this terrible thing, and I believe he should go to prison for it. But my heart totally breaks for my children, even now.*

Father, I pray you'll be glorified through it all. I ask you to guide the closing arguments, make the truth shine, and falsehood be covered so that the jurors are totally and completely clear on guilt or innocence. Father...may truth, justice, and righteousness prevail. I pray for the heavy hearts of the family and friends who are affected by this, that you would bring comfort, Lord. Thank you for all the work that has gone into this case, for all who have done their best.

CHAPTER 26

Closing Arguments and the Verdict

After both the state and the defense rest their cases, closing arguments begin, first with the state. Initially the prosecutor acknowledges the tedium of facts that the jury has endured for two weeks, and thanks them for their attention. He then repeats the court's charge to the jury, emphasizing these points:

- A person is criminally responsible as a party to an offense if the offense is conducted by his own conduct or by the conduct of another for which he is responsible, or both.

- A person is criminally responsible for the offense committed by his own conduct or by the conduct of another, if acting with intent to promote or assist the commission of the offense, he solicits, encourages, directs, aids, or attempts to aid the other person to commit the offense.

- John Howard solicited or aided Michael Lorence or another person in shooting Nancy Howard.

The prosecutor begins his argument, touching on the major pieces of evidence and the conclusions they support:

- John Franklin Howard led two lives: a loving father and husband and a loving adulterer.

- He's Frank to friends and family, and John to the criminals involved in the case.

- John's mistress demanded that he divorce his wife and threatened to end their affair if he didn't.

- Frank didn't consider divorce an option.

- Frank's children don't believe he solicited anyone to kill their mother, but they also knew nothing about his double life.

- Frank learned about Billie Earl Johnson from Chris and Christy Johnson, Billie's brother and his wife, who worked alongside Frank.

- Frank got Billy's phone number from Chris and/or Christy, and called Billie.

- Billie agreed to shoot Nancy Howard for money.

- Billie's family and friends participated in getting money from John Howard.

- Over seventy thousand dollars was wired to various bank accounts from companies that Frank created.

- Over thirteen people (including bail bondsmen and an attorney) testified they used the same number to call John.

- When "Wes" and "Tiffany" blackmailed John, he didn't contact the police; instead, he asked them to find someone to shoot Nancy.

- Witnesses' testimony is confirmed by bank records, wire transfers, hotel receipts and records, phone records, text messages, the church video, car rental records, and recorded calls to John Howard from Stacey and Billie while in jail.

- Conspirators knew Nancy's schedules and whereabouts at unusual times.

- Maps of Michael Speck's movements on the day of the shooting and phone records show that he was in constant communication with John Howard.

- Although Frank offered to do anything to find the shooter, such as offering a reward, he said nothing about the most relevant information: the identity of those involved in the shooting, such as Billie Earl and Michael Speck.

Following the prosecutor's argument, the defense makes these points:

- The charge to the jury says nothing about the people from East Texas other than that they may be accomplices.

- There is no evidence that "another person" was involved in the shooting, and the only evidence that Michael Lorence was involved was what he told Misti Ford: that he shot some woman in the head. That woman could or could not have been Nancy Howard.

- There is no evidence of "renumeration" to Michael Lorence.

- There is no evidence that Michael Lorence ever had any contact with John Howard.

- The state has not produced the phone that John Howard is said to have used to contact Michael Speck and others involved.

- The detective took documents signed in his presence to the police station to be notarized.

- Billie Earl and Stacey Serenko said their contact with John Howard began in February, 2009, but it was actually in 2010.

- There's no evidence that Howard believed divorce was unacceptable. After all, he was divorced from his first wife.

- There's no evidence of what was said in the phone calls between Howard and Michael Speck on the day of the shooting.

- It doesn't make sense that a CPA would send or give so much money to criminals to shoot his wife and not state a firm price and not even demand a bill.

- Charlie Louderman is a loon, and Dustin Hiroms is an idiot.

- Dustin said he inadvertently deleted Howard's responses to his text messages.

- The shooting occurred three weeks after Howard refused to give Billie more money.

After the defense emphasizes that the burden of proof is on the state, the prosecutor begins her final argument. First, she describes my suffering, both physical and emotional, caused by the shooting and the revelation of Frank's affair. Then she starts to construct the timelines of events:

- January, 2009: Billie gets out of jail and begins dating Valerie Rogers.

- July 4, 2009: Valerie breaks up with Billie, and about that time Frank starts working for Raley.

- July 24, 2009: Frank meets Suzanne, and they quickly begin an intimate relationship.

- August, 2009: Frank creates companies and bank accounts named after Suzanne. As signatory authority, he rapidly receives six million out of Raley's thirty-two million.

- August, 2009: Billie harasses Valerie, who tells her co-workers (Chris and Christy Johnson) and Frank about it. Frank asks for Billie's number so he can tell Billie to stop the harassment.

- After August, 2009 to early 2010: Frank calls Billie and begins giving him money to shoot Nancy.

- March, 2010: Billie is arrested and has between fourteen thousand to seventeen thousand dollars with him, left over from Frank's payment.

- March, 2010 to March, 2012: Billie, Stacey, and, for a while, Jennifer Northcutt move from hotel to hotel and jail to jail—spending lavishly, meeting Frank at various locations to pick up money and receiving wire transfers and bond money.

- September, 2011: Jennifer Northcutt is arrested and abandoned by Billie and Stacey. Northcutt tells DEA Agent Daniel Morgan about the conspiracy, even implicating herself, but the information is too thin for investigation. However, she draws a map of the house, showing where the meter box is.

- April, 2012: Billie suggests that Howard get a prepaid phone. Family members of Billie get involved. Billie and his nephew Michael Speck indicate to Howard that they will take care of business. Howard ditches his prepaid phone so it can't be traced back to him.

- April 19, 2012: Howard gets another prepaid phone, the one that connects Frank to so many of the conspirators.

- May 20 to 21, 2012: Frank and Nancy celebrate their anniversary at a bed and breakfast. Only during this period are there no calls from his prepaid phone to the East Texas gang.

- Late May, 2012: Michael Speck gets involved at the Bass Pro meeting, and the gang plans to kill Nancy in San Marcos at her mother's house.

- June 2, 2012: Stacey and Billie get arrested in Denton County. Howard stops bailing them out, says he's "all in with Michael."

- June 30, 2012: Michael Speck stops communicating with Howard.

- July 1, 2012: Dustin Hiroms, Stacey's son, gets money from Howard to "do the deed."

- July 4, 2012: Dustin meets his mother's neighbors, Jason and Stephanie, and tells them about the plan. The next day Dustin and Jason go to Carrollton and are picked up by police in the Howard neighborhood. Dustin is high and tells police he's a hit man.

- July, 2012: Stephanie and Jason start their blackmail scheme with Howard.

- August 11, 2012: Michael Speck contacts Howard.

- August 15, 2012: Speck wires a thousand dollars to Michael Lorence's fiancé, Misti Ford. Then Misti and Michael Lorence drive to Texas and rent a car.

- August 18, 2012: Speck and Lorence go "to Dallas to do some sightseeing and side jobs." When they return to East Texas around midnight, Lorence tells Misti he shot a woman in the forehead in her garage.

Following this long recitation of events, the prosecutor explains what I find most convincing: the specific knowledge that these thugs had about Frank and about my whereabouts. They knew about the affair. They knew what car I drive, the exact location of the scrapbooking retreat that I attend each year, and the house where I go to make greeting cards and the front window in the dining room, where we sit. They knew about my mother's cardiac event and my stay in San Marcos to care for her—they even knew her house.

They knew about my flat tire and my stay at the Gaylord hotel. They knew the location of my house, the blue vase sculpture in the front yard, the meter box in the back of the house, and the location of my jewelry. They knew we are members of the First Baptist Church in Carrollton and that I was going to be there on Saturday evening, August 18, 2012.

How did they know all that? Frank told them.

As for Frank's motivation, the prosecutor reminds the jury of Suzanne's ultimatum that he divorce me, our son's testimony that divorce was not an option in our family, and Frank's response to Suzanne that he knows what he has to get done. Not once does he mention divorce.

Finally, the arguments are over. The jury has its charge. The jury begins its deliberations. I wonder how long it will take for them to reach a verdict. I don't wonder for long. They reach a verdict in just under two hours. Before the jury is brought in and the verdict is read, the judge warns those in the courtroom to control any outbursts of joy or sadness.

As the jury files in and is seated, a hush falls over the room. To the judge's question of whether their verdict is unanimous, the presiding juror answers, "Yes." I focus my attention on Frank. I find myself holding my breath while the bailiff is handing the verdict to the judge, who reads the verdict: Guilty of the offense of attempted capital murder! Frank's face shows no expression, but I see his chest heaving in and out, exposing what his face conceals—shallow breathing that reveals the racing of his heart.

I'm startled by my own reaction to hearing those words—"Guilty," "Murder." Yes, it is the right verdict. But somehow hearing that twelve people agree that Frank went to extravagant lengths to have me killed also kills that hope I had hidden, even from myself: That Frank never stopped loving me.

CHAPTER 27

The Victims and the Sentence

After a brief recess, everyone files back into the courtroom for the punishment phase of the trial. I had not realized that the jury would be deciding on Frank's punishment, which meant that the lawyers would be arguing their positions again. And I would have to testify again!

The prosecutor goes first, explaining that the jury should consider not only the evidence that had been presented before but also some new evidence. As the victim, I am the first witness. Asked to describe any other health-related issues, I explain the difficulty I still have with a prosthetic eye. Because the eyelid doesn't have any muscle, the prosthetic continues to need rebuilding. I describe my daily process of washing my eye. Because it doesn't blink or close, it gets sticky. Every morning when I wake up, the eye is matted. To clean it, I first must loosen it, which is very painful. This will be my routine for the rest of my life.

I tell the jury about the numbness and weakness that I still experience in my arm. And I show them the places on my arm and collar bone where people often squeeze in a show of affection. That gesture, meant to be loving, causes shooting nerve pain from my chin to my arms. So, if someone even brushes by me, I often have to grit my teeth not to scream in agony. Being a person who likes to hug, I hate that I have lost the joy of the human touch. Even when I'm not touched, sometimes my arm will go into a muscle spasm, which prevents me from straightening it out.

Asked about any other physical damage, I tell about losing my sense of smell because the bullet traveled through my sinuses. My sense of taste has also been compromised, and I have some problem with swallowing.

Another effect of the shooting is the brain injury that is called a processing and transfer delay. I can be in the middle of a conversation or listening to some information and become "stuck" on something because I either didn't hear or didn't understand it. And the organizational skills that I used to have, especially when working as a wedding or event coordinator, have been impaired.

When the prosecutor asks how I felt when Frank told me on the phone about his affair, she may have been surprised by my response—that I was relieved finally to have an answer for his behavior toward me. Then I understood why all my attempts to bring us closer together never worked. I also say that I was angry at the police when they prohibited Frank from seeing me at the hospital—at that time I was convinced that he wasn't involved. And I continued doubting his guilt until he was indicted and I began seeing all the evidence police had gathered.

Concerning our divorce, I repeat that I filed to protect myself financially though at the time I wasn't sure that I would go through with it. Only later, when I realized that Frank wasn't just having an affair but was leading a double life, did I go ahead with the divorce. The activities of John Howard were contrary to someone I wanted to live with.

It was during the divorce proceedings that I learned about the companies Frank had set up and named after Suzanne. Again, I think to myself, maybe he hadn't wanted a divorce because it would reveal how he had used those accounts. Asked if I was given half of the valuation of those accounts or any of the real estate in California, I answer, "No." Those accounts and their use were matters between Frank and Richard Raley, which I wanted no part of.

The questions then turn to my relationships with my children, who still believe in their father's innocence. Although I understand their loyalty to their dad, I wish it was not at the expense of their loyalty to me. I hope that the strain and distance in our relationships are only temporary. I've already lost most of the relationships with my extended family, who have been such a significant part of my life. I can't bear to lose my own children.

I'm glad for the next question: Are you a spiritual person? My answer gives me the opportunity to describe the one positive result that I've experienced from this tragedy—the chance to glorify my Lord. This journey has deepened my faith in Jesus Christ, for during my many struggles with fear, he has overcome that fear with peace, peace that is beyond human understanding. Often when I become anxious in a crowd of people I don't know, I pray and recite Scripture to myself. God is always faithful to calm me in those moments. When he can use me to testify to that faithfulness, I see the truth in what James 1:2-3 says: "Consider it pure joy... whenever you face trials because you know that the testing of your faith develops perseverance."

Then the defense revives the old dance-at-the-wedding controversy by trying to force me to accuse my children of lying in their testimony: that I asked them to ask Frank to dance with me. I will not call my children liars. I can only suggest that their memories are not fully accurate. When the prosecutor asks me to explain the context, I repeat that my question was whether my daughter would like for Frank and me to dance at her wedding. My first impulse was to make my daughter happy, to see us dance as we had at her sister's wedding. Then I realized that dancing with Frank was not a good idea. I had just momentarily been caught up in the joyful celebration of the wedding.

After the prosecutor establishes my need for medication for pain and for post-traumatic stress, the defense's final questions are about the financial settlement: I receive alimony of two hundred a month, which didn't start until almost seven months after the divorce was finalized. Frank continues to pay my insurance, about eleven hundred a month. And I received eight hundred thousand dollars, which includes the value of the house. That's what our thirty-year marriage amounts to.

Following my testimony, Richard Raley is called to the stand, also to give a victim's impact statement. One of the contentions is whether Raley paid Frank a salary. Raley says he furnished Frank an office and paid all related expenses as well as any travel-related expenses. According to Raley, he promised to give Frank the opportunity to use his own money to buy into investments that Raley would make. Apparently Raley and Frank have civil suits against each other, Frank for unpaid salary and Raley for theft.

Another issue is Raley's use of hydrocodone. He is currently on probation for illegal possession of that drug. Frank's lawyers continue to hammer Raley about his drug use, contending that Raley's memory is inaccurate due to his drug use.

On the other hand, the state stresses Raley's misplaced trust in Frank, who opened accounts in his own bank with himself as the only signature authority. Raley claims that Frank siphoned money into those accounts that was supposed to go to the IRS. Moreover, two of the accounts in Frank's bank had names identical to the accounts in Raley's bank.

The machinations of all these financial transactions confuse me, but two things seem clear to me: Frank cleverly stole money from Raley, and Raley likely was guilty of tax evasion. Luckily, I don't have to be involved in any court-related proceedings on these issues. Let the judges, juries, and lawyers sort out who's guilty of what. What I've learned from all this testimony is that Frank and Raley probably deserved each other.

The first witness for the defense before sentencing is Frank's father, a retired Baptist minister. He testifies that Frank was always available when he was needed, that he visited our family frequently, and that he had never been convicted of a felony.

Our children are called next, with our younger daughter being first. Rather than being questioned, she makes a statement in support of her dad. She describes him as a great father, who has stayed in touch with her during the past two years, always encouraging and supporting her, and always speaking highly of our family and me.

Our older daughter echoes her sister's description of Frank as a great father as well as a good man. According to her, he always sends my alimony check on time and will be my main source of income for the foreseeable future. (I hope that my two-hundred-dollar alimony check won't be my primary income.)

She goes even further by asserting that Frank has done everything he could to make me comfortable: cooperating by staying away from the house when I'm there. (Of course, because he was under court order to do so, keeping his distance was in his best interest.) She also relates how cooperative Frank was at her sister's graduation and wedding—staying at a different hotel and sitting on the side of the room farthest from me. (At least I can agree with this part of her testimony.)

She ends her testimony by declaring that Frank has continued to do everything possible to support her and her siblings, me, and his parents. Finally, she asks what benefit is there in keeping him away from these obligations.

Our son is the final witness. Rather than focusing on Frank's virtues as a father, he emphasizes our family's belief in God and in grace. Describing grace as something given and not deserved, he pleads for grace to be given to his father so that he might someday be able to meet his grandchildren. With that emotional appeal, testimony ends. The state rests. The defense rests. The end is in sight. Tomorrow is the sentencing, which will be preceded by both sides' final arguments. (I hope this time the word "final" really means "**Final**.")

August 21, 2014—Sixteen days have passed since this trial began. Now we'll finally know what's next for Frank. The prosecutor asks the jury not to consider probation and not to assess a fine because it doesn't go to the victim. The options of imprisonment are either life or a range of five to ninety-nine years, the possibility of parole being half of the sentence; for life, it would be thirty years.

The prosecutor asks for a prison term that fits the crime, which he calls monstrous. Arguing that the crime was not a "one-time aberration," he declares that it took place over years. Rather than stepping back and asking "what am I doing," Frank would get frustrated and angry that nobody got the job done. Dollar after dollar he doled out (not even his own money) to as many as three different groups of people. He ends his argument by quoting from the Book of Matthew: "He who exalts himself shall be humbled." Declaring that Frank exalted himself at the expense of his children and wife, he asks the jury to humble Frank.

Countering the prosecution, the defense acquiesces in the likelihood that Frank will receive a prison sentence. However, he asks the jury to consider that Billie Earl, Stacey Serenko, and Dustin Hiroms will walk despite their participation in the crime. He does acknowledge that Billie is serving twenty-four years on federal charges and asks whether twenty-four years is the maximum sentence Frank should get. He ends by repeating our son's plea that Frank should someday be out of jail to see his children and grandchildren.

The prosecution has the last word—"betrayal," which she says sums up the case and the man. She says not only did Frank use Raley's money as a slush fund to provide lavishly for his mistress and to finance murder- for- hire schemes; he also used that money to countersue Raley. She also calls the argument for clemency to enable Frank to pay me two hundred a month "insane."

She refers to the defense's acknowledgment that Frank "got down in the gutter" with the East Texas folks, but she maintains "they aren't even on the same playing field." With those folks, you know what you're getting. They have a code, though quite foreign to most of us. Billie said he would do forty years to protect his children. Charlie would kill an Aryan brotherhood rapist, but not a sweet, innocent lady like Nancy Howard. Frank went much further. He has a cold and wicked heart. This last characterization of Frank startles me. I can hardly bear to think that description fits Frank, the husband I loved and lived with for almost thirty years. But I guess for someone who knew Frank only for the past two years, Frank is wicked and cold.

After lunch, the jury comes back with their verdict: confinement for life.

I'm stunned.

I have agreed to give an impact statement because this is my chance to speak directly to Frank and tell him what is in my heart. While awaiting the verdict, I write what I need to say. As I begin to speak, I look directly at Frank, though he carefully avoids looking at me. As I see his stone cold demeanor, I remember his telling me once that the opposite of love is not hate: it's indifference. And he's revealing it perfectly. Even if he ignores me, he has to hear me:

> *Before I read my "Dear John" letter, I want to speak to Frank. Frank, I loved you with all my heart. I was devoted to you; I served and supported you in your career and all your dreams. You told me a good wife was being a good mother to our children, and that's what I did. I loved, nurtured, taught, and cared fully for our children. You never had to worry about them; you could simply enjoy them. By example, I taught your children to love, honor, and respect you.*
>
> *You once told me your down fall was the three G's—Girls, Green, and Glory…. They got you, didn't they? You led me to believe we were working on saving our marriage by sharing in scripture and prayer. But instead, you took that love and devotion and threw it away in the shape of a small silver gun with a bullet to my head.*
>
> *You have been successful in your plan to eliminate me from your life and keep our children for yourself. But I forgive you for the lies, the adultery, and for tearing our family apart.*
>
> *Now, "Dear John," may I call you John? I know it seems personal to be on a first-name basis since I don't know you….I have one request of you. You hold a key that I would ask you to use. Take that key and unlock all the chains of deceit and lies that you have placed on our children, your family, and friends. Release them from the prison you have placed them in. Tell them the truth and take responsibility for your deeds. Give them the freedom to live in truth.*

With my final word—"truth"—the trial ends. As people begin filing out of the courtroom, we linger to avoid as much of the media as possible. I look over at the defense table, but Frank is gone. The real truth—he has been gone for over two years. Suddenly I feel empty. This does not feel like a victory at all…. The devastation to our family does not change with the verdict. Yes, it is a kind of closure, but not a celebration. I am sad beyond words.

CHAPTER 28

Trial after Trial

Now that the trial is over, I feel both grief and relief, anger and gratitude, anxiety and hope. Sorting out these conflicting emotions will take time. For now, I need to thank all those who have supported and loved me through these past two years—loyal friends and family, and especially my Lord. Even in my darkest moments, God has been faithful to raise me up. He provided an attentive jury that endured hours of testimony, objections from lawyers, and numerous trips in and out of the courtroom while points of law were debated. I'm also thankful for a wise and discerning judge; a prosecution team that meticulously organized and presented evidence; and the dogged detectives who ferreted out that evidence.

Most of all, I thank God for choosing life for me two years ago.

But what to do with my life now? That is the same question I had when our children began leaving home—who am I now that I've worked myself out of a job as a fulltime mother? Except this time, I'm not even a wife. As I consider what my next steps should be, *Dateline* finally airs the story of my shooting, precipitating another round of requests for speaking engagements as well as exacerbating the tension with my children.

But though I have temporarily lost my close relationship with my children, God begins revealing the next steps I should take by urging me to go on my first SPARK trip. SPARK, the acronym for "Serving People and Reflecting Kindness," is a ministry to women living in faith-based shelters. Some of these women have made poor choices; others are victims of abuse and abandonment by their spouses; and still others have found themselves in situations out of their control. But their common need is to know the love of God and Jesus Christ. SPARK's theme for this trip is "Identity Secured," based on Deuteronomy 33:12: "Let the beloved of the LORD rest secure in him, for he shields him all day long, and the one the LORD loves rests between his shoulders."

God's timing is perfect. He uses this serving opportunity to assure me that my identity is secure in Him. And he provides the best prescription to combat self-pity: focus on the needs of others. By giving me the opportunity to tell others about my experience, he leads several broken women to share their hurts with me, women who identify with my hurt and who need my encouragement: one woman has also been shot, and another one also has a prosthetic eye. A coincidence? I don't think so.

For now, I steel myself for the next trial, that of Michael Lorence, the shooter, or I guess I should say the alleged shooter, at least until a jury finds him guilty.

About a month before the Lorence trial is scheduled to begin, the lead prosecutor notifies me that Michael Speck, the driver, has requested a plea deal. The deal specifies that in a recorded interview he would confess his role and all the other details about the shooting. When I see the interview, I am overwhelmed by new information and answers to some of my questions. I am also surprised at Speck's calm and almost soft-spoken recital of the details. He seems indifferent to the story he is telling, almost like a normal guy recounting the score of last night's football game. Yet he is as responsible as Frank for my losses.

Watching the interview and hearing his confession help prepare me for another lengthy trial and also reinforce my confidence that Speck was not the shooter.

STATE'S EXHIBIT 286

Michael Lorence

Lorence's trial begins exactly a year after Frank's trial. In August 2015, I return to the same courtroom with many of the same participants. The one major exception is the defendant, Michael Lorence, who enters the courtroom with a confident stride. His arms are quite muscular as though he regularly lifts weights. I can imagine him in his jail cell, every day doing a hundred pushups. I doubt that any of the other inmates can intimidate him. Certainly, he seems unaffected by the circus surrounding him

As he walks toward the defense table, we lock eyes. Although I am trembling inside, I will not look away. I continue staring at him, hoping to see him react…nothing. He sits down between two of his three attorneys, with his hands folded and fingers interlocked until the judge asks how he pleads. "Not guilty." Hearing him speak those words whisks me back to my garage where I was told, "Gimme your purse." I am chilled to the bone.

Before the proceedings begin, the defense requests that I not be allowed to sit in the courtroom before my testimony. I am escorted to the victim's waiting room, where I wait for over two days of testimony. But the court reporter's account provides me with the testimony given during my absence.

After opening arguments and testimony from first responders to the shooting, Billie Earl Johnson makes an encore appearance. Most of his information repeats what he said in Frank's trial, but when Michael Speck takes the stand, he adds a couple of details that I don't remember. He recounts an occasion in which Billie received a text from Frank (or John, as he was known then) saying that I would be at Hobby Lobby. With Michael "riding shotgun," Billie drove to the store and waited in the parking lot for forty-five minutes until I came outside. Although the plan was for Michael to use the gun Billie had brought, Michael told Billie he couldn't do it. There were too many people around, and it was still daylight—too risky to take a shot.

But they didn't give up. Michael says they followed me across the street to a Wendy's and parked at a Chevron station with a good view of the restaurant. While they were waiting for me to come outside, Michael went into the station. When he saw himself on the station's camera, he hastily retreated. Another instance of being in the wrong place at the wrong time—another delay, another example of God's protection.

Michael mentions another aborted mission with Billie, to a movie theater where I was supposed to be. Although Michael looked all around, even inside the theater, he didn't find me. Now I understand why there were so many phone calls and texts from John to Billie and other conspirators. During Frank's trial, I thought I had heard everything, but from Michael's testimony, I learn more chilling details, such as the revelation that Speck and Lorence drove by my house the day before the shooting, presumably to scope out where I was to die. I wonder if I was home at the time. Will I ever stop feeling violated when I discover how often the attackers were close by?

Michael reveals that he originally planned to be the shooter, with Lorence as driver. However, because Lorence felt indebted to him for things that happened in prison, Lorence said he would do the shooting. He also told Speck that because of his young son, he had more to lose than did Lorence. Too bad Lorence's "generosity" wasn't rewarded. Neither he nor Speck received the expected payoff of twenty thousand. Moreover, the failure to kill me dashed Speck's hope for more jobs—I guess even hit men need referrals.

I also read in the court records that on the day of the shooting Speck and Lorence first went to Ross to buy wardrobes for the crime. Wow! I didn't realize that there is a dress code for murder—hoodies, hats, and red Nike shoes for the shooter. Maybe red is the required color to camouflage the blood that would spill.

That evening the suitably attired pair trailed me from the church to Taco Bueno, but on my way home, Michael reveals that they speeded past me to arrive first. According to Michael, he dropped off Lorence behind my house and then parked at the end of the alley to wait. After he heard a shot, he drove around to pick up Lorence, and they sped away to ditch my purse several blocks from the house. But after dropping the purse in a dumpster, they realized that Lorence had lost his hat. So back they drove to the house and picked up the hat in the alley.

As I read Speck's testimony, I'm suddenly struck by a new realization of God as my Shield—he protected me by preventing the felons from noticing that my garage door was down, a sure sign I was not dead. Moreover, he led me to turn off the security alarm, which would have also alerted them that I was alive. Had they known that the bullet wasn't fatal, they probably would have returned to finish me off. I think about seeing that yellow-clad arm through the glass pane in the front door and Dustie's reassurance that it was a police officer. While I had been waiting by the front door, the shooter could easily have opened the door, which I had unlocked for my rescuers before they arrived. I thank God again for sparing my life.

After retrieving the hat, Michael says they took off for East Texas, stopping on the way to buy liquor and to text John, "It's done." Remembering what I was experiencing as these villains were busy covering their tracks, I am strangely amused by Michael's statement that they didn't drink until they arrived back in Grand Saline. Driving while drinking—at least they're innocent of one crime.

On the drive home, the sober pair threw the silver gun in Lake Tawakoni and dropped Lorence's hat, hoodie, and shoes on the side of the road. A few days later, Speck phoned Lorence, who was back in California, and told him that I wasn't dead. Lorence replied, "That's impossible. I saw her brains splatter across the wall behind her." That graphic account, though erroneous, again reminds me of my miraculous survival.

CHAPTER 29

Testimony Redux

O nce more I'm called to testify to the shooting, to repeat much of what I had said during Frank's trial. However, this time there is a peculiar exchange between the defense attorney and me, comical in an perverse sort of way. When the prosecutor asks me to describe my actions after the shooting, I tell of hearing God say to me, "Get up! Get up!" The defense attorney immediately objects, on the basis of hearsay. Really! I'm flabbergasted. Did she really describe God's instruction as *hearsay*? As I glance at the jury, I detect a similar response. An awkward moment of silence is quickly followed by the judge's instructing the lawyers to approach the bench for an off-the-record conference, which I strain to hear. But I can guess the outcome because the prosecutor resumes questioning me with no objection raised to my repeating "the hearsay" from God.

After I'm excused, I return to the victim's waiting room until after the testimony of the next witness: Grady Vollintine. From the court record, I learn that Vollintine became friendly with Lorence when they were fellow inmates in a federal prison. Vollintine reveals that Lorence, who went by the name "No Good," told him that the state was saying that he shot a woman for a thousand dollars. Lorence laughed, saying "I wouldn't kill nobody for a thousand," but didn't say how much money he expected. However, he did say, "I shot that b——"

As usual, the defense's cross examination aims to discredit Grady's statement by suggesting that his motive is to get a sentence reduction in exchange for his testimony. Although I don't think Grady is very creditable, he provides another glimpse into the criminal world—apparently, inmates like to rename themselves. Lorence is "No Good" (very fitting), and Michael Speck is "Smash."

After a short recess, I'm allowed to return to the courtroom to hear the last witness, Lorence's ex-fiancé, Misti Ford. She proves to be a more credible witness as she repeats what she had said during Frank's trial: that Lorence told her he had killed me. When asked why she didn't contact the police, she explains that she was afraid of Lorence. Over the months following the shooting, he became violent, even throwing her against a wall. When she called 911, he whispered in her ear, "You might want to hang up or the same thing is going to happen to you that happened in Texas." She did finally confide in her sister, who told their mother—providing the breakthrough that the police needed. I silently thank my prayer group for all the prayers that led to that breakthrough.

A brief recess follows the prosecutor's examination of Misti. While we wait, Lorence is escorted into the holding area next to the courtroom. The wooden door to the holding area is slightly ajar, providing my brother a view of the cell. Suddenly we are startled by a shrill crash! My brother leans over to whisper to me what he just saw—Lorence's ramming his fist into a steel door that separates him from freedom. The violence in that man is scarcely contained. I wonder how many other victims have experienced the effects of that violence.

When court is back in session, the defense tries to counter the state's case by eliciting Misti's admission that Lorence felt bad about shooting a woman. She testifies that he even cried at one point over what he had done. Nevertheless, Misti continues to declare that she was afraid of Lorence. One moment of remorse doesn't change his guilt.

The final witness, Detective Wall of the Carrollton Police Department, also repeats his testimony from Frank's trial. But this time, I learn something new—how line ups are arranged. On two occasions when I was asked to identify the shooter in a lineup, I failed to identify Lorence, a mistake that the defense uses to suggest Lorence's innocence. However, when the prosecutor asks Detective Wall to explain, he describes the criteria for selecting individuals for lineups: individuals must resemble the main suspect and they must be incarcerated outside the state. Those criteria help to ensure the credibility of the victim's identification and reduce the need for tracking down persons identified by the victim but in another state. As Wall explains, if all the other individuals in the lineup looked quite different from the suspect, any identification would be unreliable.

Wall further testifies that he interviewed Lorence in California, where he was incarcerated for another crime. The video that Wall made of that interview shows Lorence screaming and denying that he was ever in Texas. But after Wall told him about the evidence, he changed his story, saying that although he was in Texas, he had nothing to do with the shooting.

With the completion of Wall's testimony, the state rests. Shortly thereafter, the defense rests, with the announcement that Lorence chooses not to testify.

The next day is filled with the charge to the jury and closing arguments, much of which I've heard before. Thinking back to Frank's trial and remembering the evidence, I wonder if this jury will also render a guilty verdict. I hope so because I've come to believe that Lorence was the person who grabbed me from behind, demanded my purse, and shot me in the head. I wish that I had been able to identify him in the lineups, but I had been so focused on that silver gun that the shooter's appearance paled in importance.

Back in the victim's waiting room, I, along with my brother and mother, hold vigil while the jury begins its deliberations. One hour passes, then another and another, already longer than Frank's jury took. Eventually we're adjourned for the day. The next day we reconvene. Finally, after thirteen hours of deliberation, the jury returns with its verdict: guilty of aggravated assault. However, the punishment phase is delayed until tomorrow because of some haggling over a missing zero in one of the cause numbers in the indictment. More lawyer talk that I don't understand or care about. I just want to get this over with.

I pray that this is the last day. I'm grateful that my son is here to wait with Mother and me. We endure more lawyer talk, this time about fingerprint analysis and the qualification of the fingerprint analyst. Then the prosecutor tells the jury the punishment range for the offense is two to twenty years, but because of two previous felony convictions, Lorence's punishment range is twenty to life. As the court instructs the jury, I learn a new term—"enhancement"—which refers to each earlier conviction. Much of the fingerprint talk seems to relate to the state's responsibility to concur with the previous convictions, each of which "enhances" the punishment range.

As we wait for the jury's verdict, I reflect on all the new knowledge I have gained during the last two years: I've learned medical and physiological terms and types of surgical procedures; the vocabulary and lifestyle of a criminal underworld; the complexity of the legal system; and the faithfulness of my Lord to enable me to endure.

My musings are interrupted. The jury has reached its verdict—sixty years.

After the jury is thanked and dismissed, I give the following impact statement to Michael Lorence:

> *You have been the force behind major loss, tragic lifestyle changes, and excruciating pain in every way—mental, emotional, physical, relational,*

and spiritual. While you may not fully understand the concept of prayer, I have prayed for you. I pray someday you will come to know the one true God, the God who is more powerful than your speeding bullet, and Jesus, the Son of God, the Jesus whose name you heard me call on as you shot me.

Because if you come to know Him, you will receive forgiveness, just as I have received forgiveness. And because I have received forgiveness, I want you to know I forgive you.

I give the same statement to Michael Speck, who received a plea deal of twelve years, but I add two sentences:

I have prayed that you will be a better father to your son than you currently are. Give him a chance in this world to not live as you have. I wish your precious son the best opportunities and that he will make wise and healthy choices as he moves through life.

After the trial ends, Mother and I head to the car. In the parking lot, we notice several jurors, whom I approach, to thank them for their verdict. They ask about my health, especially the residual effects of my injuries. My answer then, as it continues to be, is that I have learned first- hand that the body is an amazing creation. I know the truth of Psalm 139:14: "I praise you because I am fearfully and wonderfully made; your works are wonderful; I know that full well."

While I am grateful for my emotional healing, some physical effects remain. I still occasionally experience muscle spasms in my right shoulder and arm, and numbness in my forearm and fingers, though not disabling. My face, nose, and lips are partially numb, and my mouth and teeth are hypersensitive. The effects of the brain injury sometimes slow down my concentration. Although my PTSD is under control and I no longer shake when I hear sudden loud noises, being touched from behind around my shoulders and neck still elicits an emotional/physical reaction.

I've been blessed by amazing doctors who have treated me as God's creation, especially my world-renowned occularist, Dr. Randy Trawnik. Dr. Randy guided me through the painful process of restoring my "blue eyes" identity. I've almost lost count of how many prosthetic eyes he created for me. He's a true artist as well as a compassionate doctor, one I continue to see annually. Though I don't lose my "eye" any more, I still have the painful task of cleaning my eyelid several times a day. That's a permanent feature of my new life.

When our conversation ends, the jurors take pictures of themselves with me. As they hug me and say good bye, I am warmed by their support and concern. My pastor is right: God truly wastes nothing. He can bring so many blessings from acts of evil.

Epilogue

It's been more than four years since my world changed. I remember the last day in the courtroom while I waited to hear Michael Lorence's punishment, I thought about all that I had learned since the shooting. Now I also realize that I had been learning what I needed well before that awful moment that I felt a strong arm around my neck.

My experience in Zambia helped prepare me for what was to come. When I witnessed the miraculous transformation in that little girl, Eneles, I realized, maybe for the first time, the great power of the name of Jesus. Yes, I had read many scriptures that described that power, but somehow seeing it happen before my eyes made it even more real, made it instinctive for me to cry, "Help me, Jesus," when I felt my life slipping away.

Even before the trip to Zambia, God was preparing me, as early as my daddy's sudden death seventeen years ago, on a Christmas weekend. During that time, God began teaching me that he uses loss and grief to redirect our hearts and minds to him. In 2000, God prompted me to write a letter to myself using the scriptures that had been significant throughout my life. It was a love letter from my Heavenly Father, which I have carried in my Bible ever since.

Then in 2008 when I felt God prompting me to go to Zambia, I explained to him that he had the wrong girl for this trip. But knowing I needed to be obedient, I prayed and prayed, asking for an affirmation that I couldn't deny. I went to a planning meeting with Family Legacy Missions International and learned that the Camp Life theme for that year was "Jesus Loves Me" based on John 3:16. They introduced a certificate that we would give the children we would work with. We would take a picture during the week with each child in our group and glue it to the certificate. On the back of that certificate would be "the Father's Love Letter," written with scriptures, just as I had done back in 2000.

The message God sent me could not have been clearer!

Today, I have freed myself from any guilt that I had felt over our failed marriage. For a while, I was questioning how Frank could hate me so much that he wanted me dead. What did I do wrong? Then in the process of healing, I began to look at myself and at Frank as individuals. What I learned about myself was that I did everything I could to save our marriage. I was not and am not perfect, but I was committed to Frank. However, I was wrong in another sense. I had believed Frank was perfect; he could do no wrong.

I have come to realize that my deep love for Frank blurred my thinking, that no one can change another person's character; only God can.

One of the most hurtful injuries I have sustained is the tension with my children. John Franklin Howard's trial left our family in painful shreds, but, thankfully, God reconciles relationships through His Son, Jesus, the Ultimate Reconciler. Through many days, weeks, months and now years, the relationships have been healing and changing. In May of 2016, all three of my children and their spouses celebrated Mother's Day with me, with a delicious meal and many family pictures. What a joyful day that was! The friction and strain of the past seemed to melt away. I remembered only how proud I am of these six young adults and blessed by their expressions of pride in me.

Another continuing difficulty is financial. In the divorce settlement, I received some of our investments, the major source of my income, adequate only for now. After my job as a part time nanny ended, I began working part time in an office, which is providing not only a small income and new friendships, but practice for my brain and body to prepare for fulltime work. Recently I began gaining new job experience through an internship in the legal field. I hope in early 2017 to have a fulltime job.

[As this book is about to go to the publisher, I am thrilled to say I got the perfect fulltime job in late January. I am working in a legal office with fellow Christians who show me love in so many ways. The work is compatible with my few remaining disabilities , and I am learning something new every day. For the first time in many years, I wake up excited for the new day.]

Occasionally I receive a bit of additional income from the speaking opportunities that God provides. I hope to develop a speaking ministry that allows me to tell of the astonishing miracles I have experienced. I have long known that God can bring great blessings from the worst kind of evil. I now have first-hand knowledge of that truth, which I am called to share. Broken and lost souls, like Michael Speck, Michael Lorence, and Billie Earl Johnson, need to know that God loves them despite their horrific actions, and that the only source of forgiveness and peace is through Christ. Although they still must suffer the consequences of their deeds, they, like so many others, need to learn the truth of Isaiah 43:19: "See I am doing a new thing! Now it springs up: do you not perceive it? I am making a way in the desert and streams in the wasteland."

Since the trial, I have had no contact with *John* Franklin Howard although I know that he is currently incarcerated in the Allred Unit located in Wichita Falls, Texas. I have learned that both of his appeals have been denied. The closest contact I have had with Frank's family occurred a few months after the trial. On Frank's birthday, I was thinking about how difficult the day must be for his parents, especially his dad, whom I had turned to after my dad's death. When I called to tell his parents that I was thinking about them, Frank's dad answered and said they were on the way home from visiting Frank.

That brief conversation reminded me how much I missed my own dad. His death so many years earlier was the first major loss I experienced since my grandparents' deaths. Little did I know then how many losses would follow, how painful those losses would be, and how excruciating the circumstances that caused them. I was bereft until I thought of something I could regain—my own name, my daddy's name.

Changing my name required me to be finger printed. As I walked into the Denton County Jail and sat waiting for the deputy to finger print me, my heart began racing. It was unnerving to be in the same jail where John Howard, Michael Lorence, and Michael Speck had been incarcerated. I remember thinking, "So this is what it's like to be arrested." Thankfully, the deputy arrived promptly and was so kind. As she finished the job, she revealed that she knew who I was and was so happy to see me looking well. After my fingerprints cleared the FBI and the judge signed the order, it was official. I was Nancy Shore again.

When I was Nancy Shore before, I was very young and immature in my thinking about love and marriage. I wanted to believe I had married the man of my dreams and would live happily ever after. Even after our children came, our attitudes and feelings seemed to easily mesh. We loved that season of our lives. But you don't take two imperfect people and make a perfect marriage. And you can't sustain a marriage with a husband who is two people.

But these days my attitude toward Frank has softened. When I think about him, I find myself focusing more on the wonderful life we had together, both as a couple and as parents of our three children. Although the romantic love is dead, I love Frank, the father of three awesome children who have grown into amazing adults. I forgave Frank, but Frank is gone. What is left is a man I never knew. As for forgiving John and his attempts to end my life, God has given me the supernatural strength to forgive him as well.

I'm continuing to rebuild myself from betrayal, rejection and abandonment. I have grown in peace and confidence. I hold on to the promise in Psalm 32:10: "...the Lord's unfailing love surrounds the [woman] who trusts in Him." And I do!

Afterword

The writing of Nancy's story was born of our conviction that it was God ordained. The timing was also God's timing. I had recently retired from the University of North Texas, where my research and teaching centered primarily on the works of John Milton, best known for *Paradise Lost*. Thus, my academic career gave me the opportunity and privilege of sharing spiritual discussions with young adults in their very formative period of development.

While I was working, often my friends would ask me what I planned to do in retirement. They knew I would need a project, one that would allow me to use my training and embrace my passions. Wasn't I going to write a book? I wanted to, but I didn't have a story that I considered worth telling.

Although I had planned to retire in 2015, that plan was accelerated in August, 2014, (ironically, during Frank's trial) by a strong blow to my face, likely an attack linked to the so-called "knock-out game," which was popular during the spring and summer of 2014. The injuries were numerous and massive (a broken jaw, nose, orbital floor), especially to my right eye. Four surgeries and many office procedures followed. But the numbness in my mouth is permanent, which sometimes affects my speech, a disability incompatible with teaching or lecturing.

Several months after my second surgery, I talked briefly with Nancy about her injuries and their residual effects. We discovered that we had several disabilities in common, as well as having undergone some of the same surgeries. I remember her praying for me as we stood in the hall after a church service.

A year later, well into retirement with the surgeries behind me, I began casting about for what to do. I did some writing about my faith and how it had intersected with my work, but I was writing only for myself. I had no audience in mind. I joined a book club, a woman's club, and a bridge group. Two exercise classes a week and one day a week of volunteering rounded out my activities, enough to keep me busy but unfulfilled.

Then in the spring of 2016, God began to nudge me. First, I learned that Nancy was looking for a job, that she needed more income. "Coincidentally," my husband and I visited a high school friend, who repeatedly asked me how I was going to use my abilities in my retirement.

A couple of weeks later, Nancy and I happened to be walking into the church at the same time. Without really thinking, I asked her if she was going to write a book about her experience. She said she had thought about it, had been encouraged to do it, but hadn't felt able to tackle such a project. I replied that I would be happy to help her if she decided she wanted to do it. Another friend encouraged her to consider working with me. A week later, we talked on the phone for an hour and learned that God had been leading both of us to this project.

Since that time, Nancy and I have been on a difficult journey, spending many hours in conversations and in prayer for God's guidance. For Nancy, the struggle has involved much soul-searching and reliving the most painful period in her life. For me, the difficulty has been in sorting out all the complicated pieces of the bizarre plot on her life. But as Nancy has frequently reminded us both, we will not offer to God a sacrifice that has cost us nothing.

Our prayer throughout this journey has been to honor the Lord and to show that even in the darkest of circumstances, he is faithful to rescue those who call on him. Nancy experienced that rescue—over and over.

For anyone who needs rescuing, consider praying to the One who can provide it:

> *Lord Jesus, thank You for loving me and showing me how much I need You. Thank you for dying on the cross for me. Please forgive all my failures and the sins of my past. Make me clean and help me start fresh with You. I ask you to come into my life as my Lord and Savior.*

Acknowledgments

I am grateful to Eleanor Shore, Nancy's mother, for her foresight in keeping detailed notes about Nancy's suffering and recovery, beginning with those first days in ICU. Those notes have been an invaluable source of information, especially because they record events that Nancy was either unaware of or had forgotten.

Nancy and I are also indebted to the Denton County court reporter, Molly Bowers, who provided transcripts of the John Franklin Howard trial and of the Michael Lorence trial.

Many thanks also go to my husband, Bill, for his encouragement, suggestions, and patience as I spent hours collaborating with Nancy and months hogging the computer. I'm also grateful to our daughters, Allison and Meredith, for cheering me on, and to Sharon, a dear and faithful prayer partner.

Finally, I must thank Larry, my high school friend who annoyed me by asking how I was going to use my abilities during retirement. Little did he know that God was using him to remind me that there was still meaningful work to do.

. . . .*Alice Mathews*

To my momma, Eleanor Shore, I owe a huge bundle of love and thank you's. You started this journey not knowing if I would live or die. Without a second thought you sacrificed your life to help support me in becoming a whole person again. You suffered alongside of me, experiencing my pain and anguish first hand, and bore the brunt of my venting when the yelling, rage, and weeping came in full force. Thank you for listening and helping me pull myself together. Thank you for praying for me, for teaching me how to live a life of aloneness and reminding me that life would get easier. I thank God for you. I love you.

To Alice, you are a woman of great talent, wisdom, and hard work. Thank you for obediently listening to the Lord and approaching me about our coming together for this project. Your testimony and heart for the Lord made it easy for me to say yes and to trust you in this partnership. Thank you for patiently listening to try to understand exactly what I wanted to convey and then painting the pictures with the right words. Thank you for patiently waiting when the mental and emotional work became too hard and I had to take a breather. We did it! I thank God for your friendship and pray that this project has been the needed fulfillment to jumpstart your retirement! Congratulations!

I have a host of people I want to thank, but if I were to list names I would surely leave someone out. To all who have prayed faithfully, listened confidentially, and cared for me in so many ways—physically and financially—my gratitude and love go out to you! Thank you for giving of yourselves to help bring me from the deep dark hole of fragility to this new normal of strength.

Most importantly, I praise the one true God who is more powerful than a speeding bullet! To my Lord and Savior Jesus Christ who chose life for me on August 18, 2012, I praise you, for you are compassionate and forgiving, faithful and true, my refuge and strength.

. . . .*Nancy Shore*

Questions for Discussion

1. Nancy believed it important to shield her children from any disagreements with Frank? What do you think about that decision? Would it have made any difference in her relationship with them if she had been more honest? Or would it have caused other problems?

2. What do you think are the first signs of trouble in their marriage?

3. What do you think about Frank's contacting his first wife and giving her money?

4. Why do you think Frank cried so hard over the death of their family friend?

5. Which of the witnesses does Nancy feel sympathy for? Which do you feel sympathy for?

6. Which witnesses told law enforcement agencies about the murder-for-hire scheme?

7. Why was the shooting not prevented?

8. What do you find most troubling about this story?

9. What adjectives do you think best describe Nancy? Frank? Billlie Earl?

10. What do you think is Nancy's greatest loss?

11. What are Nancy's other losses?

12. How do you think Nancy endured all the suffering and losses?

13. What would you say to Nancy's children if you have the chance?

14. What, if any, humor do you find in the story?

15. What do you think are the most hurtful moments that Nancy experiences?